Circle of Years

A CAREGIVER'S JOURNAL

Circle of Years

A CAREGIVER'S JOURNAL

Houston Hodges

MOREHOUSE PUBLISHING

Morehouse Publishing
P.O. Box 1321
Harrisburg, PA 17105

Morehouse Publishing is a division of the Morehouse Group.

Printed in the United States of America

Cover design by Corey Kent

Cover art: Kactus Foto, Santiago, Chile/SuperStock—The Vigil of Angelito,
Arturo Gordon Vargas

Library of Congress Cataloging-in-Publication Data

Hodges, Houston, 1930–
    Circle of years : a caregiver's journal / Houston Hodges.
      p.   cm.
    ISBN 0-8192-1748-4 (pbk.)
    1. Aging parents—Care—United States.   2. Aging parents—
United States—Psychology.   3. Adult children—United States—
Family relationships.   4. Adult children—United States—Psychology.
5. Mothers and sons—United States.   I. Title.
HQ1064.U5H6   1998
306.874—dc21   98-14419
                                               CIP

Contents

Sandwiched In

𝒯ourteen million Americans report problems in their jobs that come from caring for aging parents. The extension of life through the use of antibiotics, advances in medical procedures and equipment, and even the reduction in smoking and the promotion of oat bran, exercise, and a healthier life style has produced some interesting side effects— including more old folks. Since "you cannot do a single thing," and everything you do affects something else, the increased supply of older adults has its impact in every area of life, from marketing to food service to publishing. Restaurants serve smaller portions for seniors, as well as for children; type sizes are set larger for older eyes; more town houses are built without stairs; pharmaceutical stocks rise; and on, and on: the Law of Unintended Consequences.

The vast increase in the "older generation" has produced enormous changes in American society and, to a lesser extent, in the rest of the world, where the proliferation of the aged has been slower. In earlier times, a senior grand-parent or great grandparent was given a place by the fire and a mat in the corner. In some societies it was the obligation of these older people to head out onto the ice floe and quietly sleep their way into history, but all has changed.

The decline of the nuclear family has spun off the elderly at the top end, so that they are no longer cared for at home. A whole industry has developed around the care of older people, with high-rises, condominiums, and retirement communities aplenty. There are new specialties in gerontological medicine, law, and social work. All one has to do is look at television to see food supplement markets that target the more mature, products that whiten their dental appliances, and disposable underwear that manages their leakage. A new specialty of personal service is the private geriatric care manager, who offers services to provide long-distance consulting advice and actual management of aging relatives. After contracting with such a service, one retiree said, "You have the paperwork and I have the life!"

Adults who are between their grown children and their aging parents have been called the "Sandwich Generation." An interconnected subculture is developing around this concept, with clubs and organizations, literature, and now web sites devoted to meeting the needs of such people. There are local and national organizations for elder care, those impacted by Alzheimer's, and stroke victims. Under the auspices of churches and community organizations there are "Caregiver's Day Out" programs and even summer camps for those with Alzheimer's—so caregivers can gain some relief from the wearing demands of being on duty day after relentless day with no respite. The four million who live under the debilitating challenges of Alzheimer's draft at least four million others to care for them; their lives are almost as deeply affected as if they had the disease themselves, plus they have an additional burden: they know all too well what's going on.

The growing literature and culture around the Sandwich Generation highlight both the blessings and the problems that accompany its distinctive situation. The blessings are evident. Members of this generation have their own past present—in the memory of a mother who sent them off to school on the first day or of a father who remembers what his grandfather was like. Such a bridge to the past is a treasure, even when memory functions have become eroded. There is an opportunity to enjoy harvest time, the closing of the circle of obligation that started life, when you were totally dependent on those who gave you birth and cared for you. Frequently at the other end of parental life there is reversal of the care transaction, and now it is you who reads to your mother or teaches your father how to tie his shoes.

Such benefits mark the Golden Years when they are truly enjoyable, if the gold in them outweighs the lead of obligation, frustration, and expense. But there is another side, as well. Guilt and obligation are twin dragons that frequently lie in wait for those of middle age (or even of retirement age) who didn't count on having this other participant, an aging parent, sharing in their retirement dream. The enormous and unplanned expenses of elder care can intrude on one's own financial planning. There are questions about insurance, complicated Medicare forms, residential decisions, and medical decisions, as well as trying to maintain as much autonomy as possible in your parent's life while still keeping him or her well cared for and safe. Tradition calls this process role reversal, when the parent becomes the child. This process is complicated by distance, however, in today's portable culture, where children live across the map or around the globe. Role reversal therefore, may be a useful starting place, but questions spread from it like water splashed from a bucket.

Perhaps the most fearsome questions lie closest to the core, to the place where life and death reside: How long will my responsibility last? When next I visit my loved parent, active on the tennis court or curled up motionless on the hospital bed, will the silent signal come for her or him to leave? Will I be ready for that? Or will this journey stretch on and on into the future, beyond a horizon I cannot probe, until I myself am old and feeble and penniless? Will I be ready for that?

• • •

This is a personal book, not a How-To. It tells the story of one particular American woman at the close of her ninth decade. Its original form was that of a journal, so most of the segments were written contemporaneously. Later it was shared with my family, and then with a supportive online community. If it can be of service, it will be in helping people prepare, helping people cope, helping people savor, and helping people hope.

Chapter One

Unfolding the New

Prelude

Betty Hodges was fine, except for those headaches. She had battled with severe migraines all her life, ever since she was a teenager. After her husband died she said that she had given them up—that she could no longer afford to have them, with a printing plant to run and a life to live.

They would really knock her out. She'd have the warning "aura" ahead of time, blurred vision and dizziness that told her one was coming. Then it hit like a mallet. She couldn't speak or eat or see. All she could do was lie there in a dark room, with a cool washcloth over her eyes, and wait it out. Every sound was painful. I learned as a teenager that when one of those migraines hit, there was no helping, no intrusive do-gooder offers of tea or aspirin, but just staying away and keeping quiet until it passed. Hours later she'd appear, ashen-faced and smiling, assuring everyone she was fine.

Most of the time when Betty said it, it was so. But despite her proclamation to the disabling headaches that they were unwelcome, they were not to be banished. Every so often, once or twice a year, there was an unexplained episode when she was "out of it," covered by her incredible coping skills and carefully concealed from all. Once she was driving back from Santa Fe to her home in West Texas; it took her four hours, maybe five. Two weeks later she told me, "It took me a little longer than usual since I stopped in a farmer's driveway for a while."

Huh? I questioned that every way I knew how, but without success. She'd slipped up once already by telling me about the mysterious interruption of the drive, and she wasn't about to let down her guard again and tell me more. I knew that torture wouldn't get her to continue the story, and besides, she was fine, right?

• • •

She'd trained at the prestigious Journalism School of the University of Missouri—in days when few women took that path. Upon graduation, the dean sent her to the wilds of far West Texas in response to his friend's plea for someone who could sell classified ads for the *San Angelo Standard-Times,* the friend's newspaper.

She met the tall young pressman early on; he was as quiet and reserved as she was bouncy and outgoing. When he invited her to dinner with his family, she wrote home afterward: "I met a nice young man and had dinner with his family. They're nice, but very poor. They had cowpeas." In Texas a homespun delight, blackeyed peas, but in Missouri they were cowpeas, fed to the cattle. In years to come I wondered that they ever got together; that they ever found anything in common, after the cowpeas episode; that they ever bridged the distance between her five-fourness and his six-foot-two, his solid quietness and her extravagant ebullience—but they did. Allen Hodges worked his way up from printer's devil to printer and won the heart of the bouncy sprite from Missouri.

I am named Houston for the man they worked for, the esteemed Houston Harte, Texas newspaper scion and one of the founders of the Associated Press.

The newspaper business in Depression times was rough, but hard work and frugality paid and kept them both employed. Their only child was born in March of 1930. They'd deposited both their paychecks the weekend the banks went bust, and their tired little automobile was sold to buy milk for the baby.

I have no idea what kind of marriage they had. He was tall, patient, taciturn, and eternally grateful that the ebullient young woman had chosen to marry him. She was busy, talkative, into everything, and never, I think, realized the treasure she had in him. I heard only one argument, ever. I heard her say, with voice raised, "How much did you lend him?" I couldn't hear his reply, but hers was quick: "You loaned Lightning five dollars, and we don't have enough to pay the bills?" (Lightning was one of the printers, nicknamed for his deliberate approach to anything.) And that was it—one in twenty years.

They worked for Mr. Harte in his sundry papers, such as Tyler, Texas (where I was born), Big Spring, Pampa, and other little towns in Texas. Then for the paper in Clovis, New Mexico, where I started high school, and then, with a loan from their benefactor, they bought the little semiweekly paper in Littlefield, Texas, with printing plant and office-supply store attached. It became the A&B, for Allen and Betty, and they loved it into growth and respectability and prizes from the Texas Press Association.

He ran the backshop. I still savor the memory of his lanky frame at the Linotype, those long fingers caressing the keys of that Rube Goldberg monstrosity. One does not tap the keys of a Linotype; all you do is touch them and they fall. Along the intricate chain of gears and levers, brass matrices fall into place, caressing the molten lead poured into a form against them, and out comes, almost miraculously, a line of (yes!) type. She ran the front—selling to, relating to, and taking care of customers. Always smiling, always planning parties and selling the supplies for them, and always serving.

Their son was supposed to be headed for newspapering, but he got sidetracked into a Presbyterian seminary and little churches. There was marriage and four wonderful children, who loved to visit their grandparents for their luxury life: swimming at the country club pool, playing in the "Grandkids' Closet" of the comfortable little house Betty planned and Allen built, and being pampered and flattered and spoiled.

Christmas of 1967, "Pop" and Betty came to Dallas to visit the new branch of the family. They went back home on the train December 27, and next morning Allen walked the length of Phelps Avenue, reporting to his cronies how wonderful the trip had been. That night came the heart attack, next morning he was dead.

After Pop's death in 1967, Betty grieved, talked to their employees, and closed the shop for a couple of days, reopening it to run by herself. She had to learn how to price printing, order paper, wheedle salesmen, and keep the printers in hand, and she did it all, through her sheer charm and hard work and gall. Once she ordered a gross of some obscure type of binder when she needed only a dozen and learned that a gross is a dozen dozen. She lowered the price, had a sale, and made money. My dad had to pay a penalty since he usually paid his bills late. Betty, however, paid them early and took a discount. She didn't know what she couldn't do, so she did it, and she never in all her life came across anything she couldn't learn, so she learned it. She ran the shop on grit and grace, made money, and then sold the shop when the time was right.

After that there were the gracious perquisites of a lady-like retirement. There was travel with her friends, cruises and trips abroad, motor tours, and driving to Dallas to the gift market or to Santa Fe to visit Barbara or attend the opera. There was filling in as a clerk at the jewelry store during Christmastime, and getting an employee discount on her own Christmas presents. At the center of her life was church, where she was the first woman elder in her congregation, and where she was chosen to be Clerk of Session, the official secretary and keeper of the minutes. Sunday school teacher, Bible study leader, and always, always the fixer, caterer, cook, and arranger of the congregation's Thanksgiving dinner, marshal of the turkeys. One of her chief delights was to take charge of getting older ladies to church. Eventually it was difficult to find anyone older than she who was not bedridden, and no one younger would ride with her—but she never stopped trying.

But the headaches. Her friends began to hint about them, word about them slipped out around the edges, and behavior began to change. Betty couldn't get her name right on her checks, kept strange things in her freezer that came off Noah's Ark, got too busy to eat regular meals, and lost things. She backed the side of the "new used" car we'd bought into a post, with one of her greatest treasures, her friend Janie Webb, at her side. Then there was the report that she had walked to the grocery store, just two short blocks away, but at twilight and smack dab in the center of the street.

I was eight hundred miles away, trying to finish up a demanding executive job in the church; trying to plan my own retirement, making a million decisions about finance and housing and relationships; and trying to find out, long distance, what was going on in that little Texas town.

She held it off as long as she could, with great coping and adjusting skills, possible only in that supportive little Texas town where everyone knew her, and where everyone knew to get out of the way when they saw her car. Her banker friend said (as judgmental as he gets), "She has her good days and her bad days." That meant to me that on some days she was a really serious case.

We put a net of coping around her: a visiting nurse, who wound up (against policy) driving her to the beauty shop; that wonderful service called Meals on Wheels, which interrupted whatever she was doing and forced her to eat a hot, nutritious lunch five days a week; and friends and neighbors, church members, her beloved pastor, and her bridge bunch, who would call ostensibly to gossip, but actually to see how she was.

I called frequently. We arranged transportation (by her yardman, at $5.00 for a sixty-mile round trip) to the nearby city of Lubbock for medical and dental appointments. I know I let her stay there in that golden, hazy dream world longer than I should have for her own good and the patience and tolerance of her community of support, but I knew (I realized but dimly) how much it would change my own comfortable and patterned life. I knew as well that for some unknown period of time it was the beginning of the new phase for her, called the End Game. I wanted to hold off its beginning in order to delay its end.

She was going to visit her friend Patsy Brittain and didn't get there. They found her sitting in her car, but on the passenger side, trying to start the engine by putting the key in the glove compartment lock. It was a really, really bad headache. Then she collapsed.

They took her by ambulance to the hospital in Lubbock, checked her in, knocked her out to make her sleep, which always helped her recover, and called me. I flew out to get her out of the hospital and take her home. It was then that the decision was made that she had to move.

In this segment you'll meet the wonderful people of Littlefield, Texas, who took it upon themselves to care for Betty after they began to notice she was having problems. Such a ministry was not given to Betty alone, since it has been extended to hundreds of people through the years. Providing a safety net for those in need is one of the things that small towns do best. You'll hear about Betty's friends: bridge buddies Ginny, Rene, Ethel, and heroic Janie Webb, who refused to give in to the stroke that knocked her off her feet, and Patsy Brittain, Thelma Reagan (now Baldwin), Tena Wicker, and Myrle Sumrall. You'll meet Betty's best friend, the indomitable Susan Wilemon, and Jimmie Woolever, who took a job as "senior companion," but turned it into friendship. A special coffee pal was Evelyn Reese, who lived close enough for Betty to walk to her house after driving became a risky adventure. And here, too, are Vada and Ben Crawford, who open hearts as well as locks. Here's "Mr. Joe" Blankenship, pushing eighty himself, who was a fine next-door neighbor. There is cousin Ninia Smith, Betty's brother Don's daughter, smitten by polio in nurse's training. She finished the training, was capped and all, and served valiantly and learned. From her college in Kansas she became a leading authority on the education of those with mobility impairment.

Here are the rest of the Hodges, always there, without whom I could not be me and probably could not be at all. Always just between the lines is the incredible love of my wife, Pat, who paid a price for everything invested in my mother. Here are my four children, afar: Bruce, who is in New York City; Christopher, who is in Philadelphia with Shaune; John and his wife, Cindy, who are in Bay City, Texas, with their two children, Rachel and Jarred; and Susan and her husband, Jim Ramlet, who are in Minneapolis. You'll hear about their mother, Barbara, my first wife, in her favorite place in the world, Santa Fe.

You'll find Wyndham Park here, a fine retirement complex in Huntsville. On one of our trips to Huntsville, my mom and I had surveyed the two most likely places. With only moderate pressure, she was persuaded to choose

Wyndham for her future residence, well before she ever thought she'd have to move there.

You'll hear about some Presbyterian churches as well, and even the denomination's national annual meeting, the General Assembly, which meets for a week each year. These churches were the bailiwick of Betty and her son after she took a nice Methodist boy and turned him into my stalwart Presbyterian father. The name of the denomination does not matter and could well have been any of a hundred others where kind people come together to worship God and to befriend those who come in contact with them.

Involuntary Alabamianism, April and May 1992

APRIL 9, 1992

I told my mom on the phone tonight about her move to Huntsville, and it was all right. She was trying *very* hard to be okay about it, and her doctor was wonderful today when he saw her. This was Dr. Jenkins, the psychiatrist, who runs a rehab center and to whom she was referred for testing. I'd talked with him last week about options. Mom liked him, too, saying "He's not like a doctor, more like a friend. He said most of my problems were caused by my age, and that's right. He said he wasn't going to give me any prescriptions, but he did want me to do one thing: he wants me to come see you."

So we talked about that. The doctor told her it wasn't permanent, just to see how it works, and I could affirm that with her. When I go get her we won't sell her house, I'll get what she needs and we'll close it up and do other stuff later in the summer. If Wyndham Park doesn't work, we will make another arrangement, but it will not be back in her home in Texas. She asked good questions—about her church, her car, her house—and then said she'd let me know when she could come. I told her I'd have to fit it in with my schedule, but we have an apartment for her as of the middle of May. So I think I'll go out for Mother's Day with her in her church, then she and I will drive here in her car. I said maybe I'd give her $10.00 for her car. She said, "How about two?" I allowed as how we could negotiate and bargain some.

She was really in pretty good shape mentally; she asked good questions, heard my answers, and let them make sense to her. I'm feeling better than I have for some days, ever since it became clear that she had to come here. She is at least beginning to work the process in a helpful and responsive way, and I am very glad.

April 11, 1992

The arrangements for my mother's move are taking a lot of time and energy. More energy than time probably, and occupying most of my emotional space, leaving the presbytery with the remnants. I am somewhat holding the presbytery's tasks at bay with one arm, while the major action is taking place in Littlefield and at Wyndham Park in Huntsville, in an effort to move one gallant and confused little old lady from the first to the second. I'll fly to Lubbock on May 8, spend Mother's Day with mom in church in Littlefield, then ship some furniture and belongings to Huntsville, and load her car with her clothes and some personal things (and her!). Then we'll drive eastward to her new life. Arrival and move in will be about May 15. The timing is pretty good. I'll have most of the rest of May in town, to help in transition, before I go to Milwaukee for General Assembly (with a weekend in Minneapolis with Susan and Jim before that).

This weekend the task is to get her to talk to her friends and her church about the move. She's so hesitant to do that, since it will mean that she's really moving. She wants to see the move as temporary, as it is, and to retain some of her autonomy, which means so much to her. But she won't be back in her house in Littlefield, I'm sure. I'm not going to make major changes in her house when I go to get her, just take furniture she'll need in Huntsville. I may put some valuable things in a secure storage facility, if there is one there. A couple of my kids—Susan and maybe her Jim, and John and Cindy—have offered to come out and help with the house, and I think they will. Barbara Hodges, my first wife, will take the beautiful Heywood-Wakefield dining room suite. I may go back to help with distributing the furniture and things worth keeping, perhaps to preside over an estate sale, and then to clean out the rest, giving it to the Salvation Army or Goodwill. Then I'll place the house on the market. May have to rent it, since I don't have any idea about the market there. And there are a thousand decisions, most of which are just guesses. I have to do the best I can with what there is to work with. Does she bring her king-size bed for her small apartment, or the double bed from the guest room, which Susan would really like? Which chest of drawers? A couch? An easy chair? Which TV? Which telephone? The one with big numbers she can dial more easily or the one with smaller keys that can be programmed for one-button dialing? Can I find the instructions for the one-button dialing? Who'll mow her lawn? What about the family heirlooms—the milk pitcher my grandmother got for a wedding present, the two vases that came from St. Louis, Aunt Gina's netsuke? Big changes ahead in the next two months for a woman who had hunkered down in her bunker and hoped to make it through from that location. Big changes for her son as well.

APRIL 12, 1992: *A Bad Day*

Mom confessed on the phone that she had a bad day; it just slipped out. It turns out that when Judy Lee came to get her for Sunday school, she came in her pickup and the heavy door cut my mom's leg. They had to go to the hospital where "a Filipino doctor sewed it up, six stitches (with black thread)," and she missed Sunday school *and* church. She did get there in time for the luncheon after church, at ten minutes to 12:00. She arrived home at 3:00 and got Jim Tom to take her to Patsy Brittain's for her usual late Sunday afternoon pastoral visit, which consisted of taking her the church bulletin and sharing a glass of wine, and then she went home. Her leg hurt, and she was going to take a pain pill sometime. I urged her to do that before she went to bed. It broke my heart when it turned out she was sorry she had called it a bad day and said, "I wanted to tell you on my own, in my own time." I asked, "Is this a good time?" and she said, "Yes." It's like a kid who's misbehaved and doesn't want to be told on, but wants to tell the parent herself. She wasn't bad, she just cut her leg. But she knows that's a black mark as to whether she's responsible or not.

I asked if she's telling people about her coming to see me. She said, "Yes, but I'm spreading it pretty thin." It's all over town, of course, since Susan Wilemon knows.

MAY 8, 1992: *Red Dots*

Uneventful trip from Alabama to Texas, smooth and on time. I slept most of the way, probably in denial that I was coming, or to rest up, whichever. But it couldn't hurt. She and Mr. Joe met me at the Lubbock airport. She had a big splotch on her blouse, where she'd found a spot just before they left and had tried to sponge it off, but it hadn't sponged.

When we got to Littlefield we were going to take Mr. Joe for tacos, but her car battery was dead—the fine new battery in the car that was serviced this week. So we went with Mr. Joe. The tacos were good, and his battery charger is working on the car.

There are supposed to be red dots on the furniture that's going to Huntsville, so every time I sit down to do something she gets the red dots and puts more of them on junk. I know, I know, it is junk that is her life.

I did find the car title and the license receipt, so I can buy the car from her. Now if I can just get it to run.

There is so much to do, and it's like swimming in molasses. But we'll get it done, red dots and all. She is very concerned about who gets what, and it is very confusing to have these treble decisions going on—what to take, what to leave, and what to give away. And when.

• • •

There is a breakfast at the church on Sunday, which I think is in Mom's honor. If it isn't, I'll tell her that it is.

MAY 10, 1992

What a day. We both worked like field hands and got an enormous amount of work done. The house in a shambles, but we had a lot of togetherness. It was 8:30 Saturday morning when she said to me, "I wish you'd get off my back!" and she was right. I was being far too paternalistic. All she wanted to do was stop to look at some old photographs when she was supposed to be getting dressed.

She is in really good shape—alert, talkative, energetic, and helpful. I have nightmares about what this task would be like if she were not helpful, but she is cooperative, agreeable, and positive. Every so often she just flat out balks about my throwing something away. The eight hand-painted daisy coffee mugs *will* go, and they'll be on the bottom shelf of the glass curio cabinet. That pack of paper napkins *will* be in her chest, so she can entertain the little old ladies who will come to see her new apartment. I try to say yes to those, so she'll have herself as much as possible. After all, I am uprooting and turning forty-seven years of her life topsy-turvy, forty-seven years of what she's collected and treasured. We're in lifeboat mode: six sets of towels, hand towels, and washcloths, four plates, four glasses, and four bowls, instead of the cabinets, closets, drawers, and nooks full of stuff.

Loads of history along the way, photos and letters and news clippings. She's an old newspaper person, and a good one, so she clipped *everything*. She has all the graduation programs for each of the grandkids and the playbills from each school play they were in. She has all of my letters to her, for the past ten years, neatly bundled, with worn-out rubber bands that pop every time you move a stack.

But it's going well, and if people will just leave us alone we'll get it done by Wednesday, when the mover comes. She wants people to come, of course, so she can cling to them and tell them good-bye and not let them go. I want to get rid of them so I can get back to those damn boxes. There is such love and sympathy in the eyes and voices and hugs of those who come by. A favorite cousin, Ninia, came yesterday, on her crutches, from her 1947 polio siege. She was consulting in Amarillo on special education. She drove two and a half hours just to see my mother. She stayed for two precious hours, taking us to the funky little Main Street hamburger place for lunch, and then turning around to get back to Amarillo for a 4:30 appointment. She says she'll come see her in Huntsville, but it may well have been the last time they'll see each other.

I keep thinking that for *her*, and she has given no indication she's aware of it, but I know that drumbeat goes on underneath: Last time. Last time. It started when we left the Lubbock airport, and went through the tollbooth from the parking lot. I realized this was very likely the last time she'd do that. Thelma Reagan came by yesterday to get some knitting books. She used to work for mom. I could tell by her teary eyes that she knew what we were doing: Last time.

And today at mom's church will probably be Last Time. The men are fixing Mother's Day breakfast. Two people have called to ask, quite casually, if we're going, so that means there's some kind of to-do for my mother. I went by yesterday afternoon to get her corsage. Last night she carefully chose a bright, colorful multicolored suit—red, green, and blue—ready to go into center ring when the spotlight comes on. Last time, and chin up.

MAY 10, 1992, LATER:

We'll make it, and we'll leave Wednesday with what we've got packed. She can just make do even if we get to Alabama without some stuff, like a banjo on our knee. But there'll be a lot. I have to look at all the clothes and spot those that are soiled, so that Jimmie, her senior companion, can wash them tomorrow. Much of the jewelry is broken, doesn't have backs on pins, or has only one of the pair. The residue of a forgetful little old lady. But I have the two gold wedding bracelets in my suitcase for Susan and the daguerreotype locket for Rachel. Mom wants to give the most precious of all, her screenlatch rose gold bracelet, to Cindy after she's worn it a while longer. So I really feel good about that. The sterling flatware is in a chest in an aluminum suitcase. We'll take that in the car.

Religion interferes with what needs to be done sometimes, and in Littlefield, Texas, on Mother's Day, religion (the local manifestation of same) is predominant. We needed to pack, right? So we went to the Mother's Day breakfast at 9:00, Sunday school at 10:00, church at 11:00, out to eat at Pizza Hut at 12:30. We didn't get home until 2:00. Then at 5:00 took the church bulletin to Patsy Brittain, who's homebound and counts on my mother to come see her. Home at 6:00.

Between religious festivities, we did get a little packing done, but I found my helper flaked out on me this afternoon. She was in real denial, full of diversions, delays, sidetracks, questions, and undoing what I'd done. I had a whole shelf of rags put up, the linens too ragged to move, and the next thing I know she had them stacked up ready to pack. Picking stuff out of the trash and telling me she *had* to have it in Huntsville, looking at stuff she'd rejected before and deciding she wanted it, and stopping on her way to everything to look at the nearest distraction at hand. And, if there was anything on a label or tag, wanting to read it to me.

The trunk to her car will not, repeat, will not open—not with any of the three keys that are supposed to work it, upside down or right side up. So add a trip to the locksmith tomorrow, to the places already planned: the bank, the post office, and the courthouse, to transfer the title to the car. And packing.

But we'll make it.

• • •

The people at her church fixed up the fellowship hall with fresh tablecloths and decorations after the breakfast. When she asked about it, they told her they were setting up early for the graduation luncheon next Sunday, and she was impressed with their foresight. So after church, wonderful pastor Jon Riches asked her to go back to the fellowship hall. She went, all suspectingly unsuspecting and trying to look innocent, and it was a reception for her, with speeches, lots of hugs from the little girls who love her, and a presentation of a new color TV set.

That's when I found that the trunk wouldn't open, thank goodness. I had to get Judy Lee to take the new TV over to the house in her wagon.

If something can go wrong, it will. But we are going to make it.

May 11, 1992

Got some more clothes loaded—about a million scarves, lots of bras, and very few underpants. I think we're going to find a sale at the nethergarment store when we get to Huntsville. I shouted at her one time, when she kept telling me that those shoes were supposed to be with that dress, and I told her for the sixth time that the shoes were in the shoe drawer and the dress in the dress drawer. But she kept on insisting, and finally I shouted at her, and she laughed and took it very well. My, my. And I told her I'd try not to shout tomorrow.

• • •

I heard her rustling in the hall, pitch dark, 6:30 A.M.; she was up, running on high. A little goofy, but lots of energy. May it redound to the glory of the packing boxes. Today will be a barn-burner: bank, locksmith, police (to let them know she's leaving her house), realtor, and the courthouse.

Jimmie, the senior companion, comes and will, I hope, wash clothes. Meals on Wheels will deliver her lunch. But with a 6:30 start, can anything stand against us?

• • •

The reason the trunk wouldn't open was that she didn't have a key for it. Simple as that. The yellow pages give the nearest locksmith in Levelland, seventeen miles away, but mom remembered Vada's husband who had worked on locks some. So I called Ben Crawford this morning at 7:30. He was here at 8:15, took one look at the car, and left, apparently to get some new or more Chryslerish paraphernalia, though I thought it probably meant he'd declined the job.

He came back in ten minutes, consulted with me, drilled the cover off the lock, and remembered to ask me if the thing had a release inside the glove box. It did, and the trunk popped open, but there was still no key for it. He took the lock off the door, left in his pickup with it, and came back an hour later. He then reinstalled the lock and handed me two new keys, which work like a charm.

All this, mind you, at molasses pace. He's seventyish, tall and bulky, and moves with the painful slowness of three crushed vertebrae from a bad fall in WWII: "But I thought the fall out the winder was better than those four Germans coming in the door." Once I said, at his deliberateness, when picking the lock wasn't working, "I can take this to Lubbock if I need to, Ben, if you don't have the kind of tools to do this." He shot me a glance of steel. "I've got the tools."

When he finished, three hours, keys, and various other bits of arcane hardware later, I asked, "What do I owe you?" He asked, "What's that in your hand?" It was my billfold. I said, "Just to pay you for your time and materials, the keys and all . . ." He said, "Put that up." I put the billfold up. "Now give me five," he said, hand stuck out. I took his hand. He looked at me without a smile: "If I can't help a neighbor when they're in real trouble, I was born on the wrong planet."

On his way back to the camper he couldn't help adding, "I could tell you were worried when you said that about going to Lubbock. But I had the tools." There was perhaps a bit of a grin as he climbed painfully into the cab.

• • •

Twelve-hour days are sometimes tiring, I've found after throwing more of them in a row than I usually do. At 6:30 this morning, she roused me, and now it's 11:00 at night. Except for a lovely oasis dinner with Ginny and Maurine, we hit it all day long. But I did the whole drill of bank, police station, realtor, post office, plus, of course, the trunk lock.

And Jimmie Woolever, who is supposed to put in two hours, was here from 10:30 until 5:30. That's a pretty good two-hour stretch. She cleaned out the pantry and the freezer. All that tiger shrimp in the dumpster, and only ten years old. Hell, those things would have been as big as lobsters if we'd let them keep on growing.

We're going to make it: the only essential left is cosmetics and toiletries, with a little extra space for clothes. Susan Wilemon is coming over in the morning to help with both, and to take clothes back to her house so Lee can wash them. The movers may be coming as early as 3:00 tomorrow to pack and load. We can get them then and, if we wait until Wednesday, they may not get here until afternoon, but we can be ready tomorrow if need be. I ought to be able to find out with an early call tomorrow.

May 12, 1992: *Moving Eve*

I woke at 5:00, but stayed in bed planning the day for awhile. I think we can do it. Susan Wilemon will be a help, and she can get my mother to cull the enormous supply of bottles, jars, vials, and tubes that keep her beautiful, most of which are empty. Got to get them into a box and a small suitcase.

Found wonderful historic stuff last night under her bed—all the pictures of her childhood, my uncles when they were boys, and so forth. Lots of 75-year-old photos.

She continues to be of good and optimistic spirit, even when I get irritated. She is really doing this whole thing in a better frame of mind than I am. Darn.

We'll spend the night here, even though the place will look devastated with her Huntsville stuff out. I need to warn her about that.

Chapter Two

Fight Against the Fog

Prelude

The headaches, of course, were little strokes, or transient ischemic attacks, abbreviated TIAs for those in the elder care game. Each time one occurs there's a momentary gasp of a blood vessel in the brain, a twitch or a spasm or a momentary blockage, preventing the crucial flow of blood to the brain. The immediate consequence is a headache, perhaps disorientation, and sometimes a loss of the ability to speak or walk or think. The long-term effect is more serious: part of the brain shuts down and stops working. Afterward there are enormous, massive, incredibly heroic efforts to fire it up again, to throw synapses around the blockage, to route the signals other ways. Sometimes it works, sometimes it doesn't; but bit by bit abilities are damaged, capabilities reduced, and options narrowed.

The result is called dementia. What a sad and archaic term for it. As far as I know, no one has come up with a more palatable name for this condition; no doctor has given her or his name to that syndrome, no politically correct revision to its bare ugliness: senile dementia. I saw it first on a doctor's chart with an assessment after one of Betty's hospitalizations: mild to moderate dementia.

It seems to be different from Alzheimer's. The Alzheimer's Society says that scourge is always fatal, but takes from three to twenty years to achieve its goal. With its cousin dementia, there's no fixed fatality and no time frame. It simply knocks off capability and ability bit by bit, nipping and nibbling arbitrarily at what you used to do so well. And that's what Betty's got.

In this segment you'll find out more about Wyndham Park, Huntsville's premier retirement facility, with sprawling wings, three full floors, and probably seventy-five little residences—miniaturized versions of the farmhouses, town houses, condominiums, and estates in which these people once lived. There are three levels of care in keeping with the modern trend. Independent Living is just like a college dormitory, but the other end of the chronology line. Coeds aged seventy-five to one hundred come and go as they wish to parties, dances, and outings; eat what meals they want; and can cook in their rooms. The few guys there are in shorter supply than any place other than at an Ivy League women's school. Assisted Living is the second level, with more help from the attendants in getting up and dressed, taking medicine, and getting to meals. Then there's Nursing Care, level three, which is through the swinging doors to Parkview, and is the dread of all those in levels one and two. "You don't come back from Parkview," they say. Although they're wrong a significant number of times, the word is still out.

Betty spent a few days with us in our condo while her furniture arrived and I arranged it in her freshly painted apartment, number 231, "down at the end of the hall, so you'll get good exercise walking to and from the dining room." Then I moved her in and left her for the night, all alone in the ultimate aloneness of the hundred other people who now surrounded her.

This is the segment in which Pat Hodges, my beloved and (mostly) patient wife, begins to show up in her invaluable role. However, it is a delusion that it is sheer delight to be beloved by two beautiful women at the same time.

You'll also hear more about those Presbyterian churches. To those not afflicted with an affinity for this interesting breed, explanations (and possibly apologies) are in order. During the first part of Betty's residence in Huntsville, Alabama, her son was finishing his job as the Executive Presbyter of a cluster of thirty-six Presbyterian churches, arranged into North Alabama Presbytery. Executive Presbyter work involves a lot of visiting those churches, knowing their pastors and leaders, and attending flocks of social events, at which Betty was an expert and of great assistance. It takes a lot of smiling.

MAY 13, 1992: *On a Road*

The sun is shining, and we've had a good day, maybe even a great one. Packing and loading went as scheduled, smoothly. I got the car serviced this morning while the movers were working and found that it needed new spark plugs. I feel much better about being on the road with it, with its oil, filter, and plugs in shape. We had a great four hundred miles, after leaving at 1:00, with not a cross word. She was admiring of the highway ("My, how well this highway is constructed") and the view ("But I like it flat"), and we had good talks, agreement, and togetherness. She was game to drive until 8:00, which meant Oklahoma City, and that was about what I hoped, if we had a noon departure.

Susan Wilemon and Joe Blankenship were there for our leaving. Susan said she couldn't bear to think of us driving away with no one to wave at us, so both of them waved as we backed out of the driveway and headed toward Spade and the rest of the new existence after Littlefield.

She didn't shed a tear, though I was gravel-throated, crack-voiced and sniffling all morning. We walked around the house one more time, and she walked out without a backward glance. But when Susan Wilemon tried to put mom's shoes in the car for her, she balked: "I'm not ready to have them go, and *I* want to take them out when I'm ready." Of course that was right, since she needed to be in control of that. Later today she said, "I can't start depending on you for everything." And I agreed. So after we got to the motel and were going out to eat, at 8:30, she had to change her blouse, since she didn't want to wear the one she'd worn in the car all day. She combed her hair and put on fresh lipstick, and then was embarrassed when we got to the restaurant and she found two drips down the front of her new blouse. The paper napkin she tried to sponge them off with simply left lint on the spots. Ah, ah. How the mighty have fallen.

MAY 14, 1992: *The New Home*

Home again—685 miles today, which is quite a drive. Good trip. I made her go too far today, but I just had to get home.

MAY 30, 1992: *In Wyndham Park*

A pretty good day. A flurry this morning when I went to pick her up. One of the housekeepers beckoned me outside and told me, "She wandered off yesterday—was out at Max Luther Drive and was going over to the beauty shop to get her hair cut since she said they wouldn't take her at the shop here." That is close enough to being true, and none of the housekeepers knew she didn't like the beauty shop in the complex. When I asked her about it, she denied it totally. She'll get killed crossing Max Luther Drive. There's a hill to prevent full view, too much speed, and no crosswalk.

She also went to breakfast downstairs in the Camellia Room, although she's supposed to eat in the Azalea Room. She told me there wasn't any room for her, but a nice girl made room for her. Whether they're supposed to or not, who knows? The director of Assisted Living comes back Wednesday, and maybe we can get together with her then. So mom said, "It reminded me of Fulton, Missouri." That meant what they called "the insane asylum" when she was there as a girl; she used the word inmates, and talked about the "surveillance." And then she said, "Maybe this isn't the right town for me," and went on about how she doesn't like to be dictated to.

So this is the first major flurry, and I pray to God we can handle it. Got to. I cannot spend all my free time with her. She has to be able to make it days and weeks on end by herself, with all the folks we are paying to keep an eye on her.

• • •

She's at our condo this evening. She and Pat are watching "Murder She Wrote." I'll take her back to her apartment after that—and try to keep her off the street tomorrow. I've promised her a walk, so we can scope out the grounds, and then I will help her buy a baby present for her great-grandson Jarred, so maybe that will keep her being good.

• • •

We went to Hope Church today. An interesting drive. She was fixated on scenery, said twenty times, "That's beautiful!" On the trip to Alabama it was "Green!" again and again. She said that a few times, too, but mostly just "Beautiful!" She told Ed Hamlett (the interim pastor at Hope) that three times, twice when she met him and once when we left. That seems to be the safe subject now; she can carry it off and not worry about goofing, as long as she concentrates on green landscapes. Who's to argue?

My mom finished the day feeling confused and discouraged, but said, "I think I'm still working at it," and I agreed. After I took mom home, I had a run-in with Pat for agreeing to go get Betty tomorrow. That was justified, since I hadn't done the planning with Pat but had instead utilized my hangover only-child method of deciding things unilaterally. I cannot do this by myself. I must not only let people help me, but also bring them in on the process. I will learn how to make it work better, though. I can do that.

JUNE 20, 1992: *Pat's Birthday*

A Saturday, and a Saturday off in the midst of the maelstrom that is 1992. Pat and I are going to relax at home; we're planning to venture out this afternoon to see "Patriot Games," the only thing passable as a movie for the AARP crowd, and will go out to eat this evening. I'm doing some Bible study in Birmingham next week, will work on that, and polish the sermon for tomorrow. I am *not* going to get my mother today, though she knows I'm off. "This is a test, repeat, this is a test," to see how she does without my going to get her, so Pat will not have that to look forward to every day I'm off. I'll call mom a couple of times, yes. Tomorrow I'll take her with me to Maranatha, the presbytery camp, as I lead worship with Fellowship Church, our wonderful black congregation.

Next week it fires up again in earnest. I have three days in Birmingham, a day in the office, and then to Littlefield for five days of grunt work and tear work, gleaning and cleaning my mother's house. The first part of it I'll have Jim, Susan, and John to carry me; the last part of it I'll be by myself, with faithful Fannie Mae (who works by the hour and cares by the year) to help with the cleaning. John and Jim both will have trucks to carry off what is salvageable. We'll discard a lot—*a lot.*

Then I come back to presbytery council and the presbytery meeting on July 21, then a week with the seventh and eighth graders at the camp. So the next month will be a rompin' stomper.

But I shall make it, I declare. There are a couple of nice bits in the middle: Chris Hodges coming to see his grandmother over July 4th weekend and my cousin Bob Hodges (my only cousin on that side) coming the 20th for a week, while his wife Gloria is at Space Camp here in Huntsville, as a Texas teacher chosen for special duty.

My stomach doesn't hurt thinking about all of it. I'm determined to do it well, thoroughly, and with some grace, even taking care of myself along the way, through rest, exercise, and wresting some hours off along the Kingdom way.

• • •

My mother has shown a few signs of better adjustment. I worked things out this week with the beauty operator, so mom will get her hair cut next week. She received the new address labels I got her and was glad to get them at her new address. I said to her Friday, "I liked coming out today for lunch and a little visit. We got some good stuff done." She said, "And that's why I'm here, isn't it?" And I said, "Yes, it is, so we can be closer together to do good stuff."

JUNE 21, 1992: *A Little Tremor*

I should have known that something was not right when I went to pick up mom Sunday morning, but she's been doing so well, and we always want to pretend her lapses are temporary, passing. She had no lipstick on, her hair was poorly combed, and she had on ridiculous indoor sport slides, instead of her sturdy walking shoes, to spend the morning outdoors at the camp. It took her several minutes to do these tasks because she was distracted between each.

During the drive and at the camp she did fine, sturdily walking a half-mile to the worship spot down by the lake, and then gladly accepting a ride back to the dining hall afterward. At lunch, when I held out a chair for her, she took the one next to it. She took hardly any food, a chicken wing when she had her choice of the pieces, and a little dollop of mashed potatoes, no bigger than a walnut, plopped at random on the plate. Beans were the big problem. She put her fork into the bean plate and tried to scoop beans onto it with the serving spoon. I helped her after watching her struggle a couple of swipes. She liked the whipped Jell-O salad; she took two spoonfuls and then put the serving spoon in her mouth and licked it off. I put the spoon firmly down on her plate. The woman next to her had noticed; she moved instantly and smoothly to cover, saying, "Let me get another spoon," and found an extra teaspoon to put into the Jell-O, so it was okay.

She stopped talking. I should have noticed, but *I* was probably talking—a family trait. When we were ready to go, she tried five or six times to hoist herself up but her legs simply wouldn't push her up out of the chair. I told her to wait while I went to get the car and drove it up the hill to the dining hall. She and Pat were walking out, slowly but steadily. Then, in the car, she began confusing words, talking strangely—slurring word-ends, and saying words that sounded right but were wrong.

Back at her apartment, forty-five minutes later, she can't speak coherently, though the cadence and rhythm and emphasis are there, like an English sentence run through a scrambler. Questions are questions, and statements are statements, but you just can't understand a word of them. I put her to bed and began the wait. She slept a short while, then woke and lay there trying to say things up to the ceiling, evidently amazed that they didn't come out right. I told her I was thinking of getting someone to look at her. She was visibly upset, but the other-world speech held a clear objection to receiving any special treatment whatsoever.

It took three hours this time for recovery to begin: "Okay!" she said, and then, "It's awful!" She got up and put on a fresh gown. I changed the sheets. She sat in her chair, began sipping a cup of coffee, wanted nothing from the tray that was brought for her. Shook her head, began repeating what I said: "You're getting better." "I'm getting better." "You'll feel better in the morning." "I think I'll feel better in the morning." She wondered what happened and was amazed when I told her.

I told the housekeeper down the hall, who said they'd keep a special eye on her. I'm going out this morning for lunch with her. I think recovery will have continued, if the pattern from the past holds.

We saved another terrible hospital bill, where they could have done nothing for her except put her to bed and wait. It was so much better to have the up-front and personal terror of watching it happen, even when not knowing how to stop it, instead of having it happen half a continent away. And I am grateful for that intrusive, high-priced, nosy institution she lives in for being able to put some care around her when she needs it.

AUGUST 5, 1992

A good half-day with my mother today. I stopped by for lunch with her—a not-so-hot lunch, just like she tells me. They usually do better when I'm there, but it was overdone charred crab cake, overdone wimpy broccoli, and a cold cheese biscuit, not well served. But not customary, thank goodness.

Then we had the afternoon together. I glued the drawer on her desk and fixed her medicine for the week. Then she wrote letters, about ten of them, using my dictating machine. I'd sit there and manage it, turning it on and off as she waved her hand at me, while she leaned up close to it and talked to her friends. Very interesting to see her think, since she really couldn't manage to conceptualize the challenge of the recorder. She couldn't realize that she hadn't said something to the next friend that she'd said to the first, and she is not ready to manage the concept of boilerplate—repeated material that is included in each letter. But I will do the letters and they'll get out, and her friends will be ever so glad to hear from her.

Then we listened to a wonderful cassette tape from about 1968—a conversation between her and her two older sisters, from Potomac, Maryland, in prospect of a trip to New York the next day to see the Broadway plays. They were figuring the bus trip at $9 each way, hotel at $17.50 per night for the three of them, and plays that would be at least $5 each and maybe even as much as $6! Such fun. We both had a little nap while we listened, and when she woke up she opened her eyes wide and said brightly, "Have you been here long?"

Then, on a little walk, we talked about her schedule for the weekend, which is rather busy. Afterward it was time for me to leave. But it was a good time. She was in good shape, making sense, and it was a delight. I need to be able to remember this day, because I know I'll need it in the future.

• • •

Pat and I are taking some vacation time next week, though technically I don't have any left, with all the time I've spent in Littlefield. I'm taking a week anyhow, and Wednesday we'll drive up to the Cumberland Plateau in northern Tennessee, to the Cumberland County Playhouse to see "South Pacific," and then to Oak Ridge to the Atomic Energy Museum and some other low-pressure sites.

I'm ready. I'm ready.

August 9, 1992: *Sunday Surprise*

I was all set to teach Sunday school at Covenant Church. I knew how much my mom would enjoy being there for that, but when I went to get her, she was lying on the floor, semiconscious. She had obviously been heading for the bathroom but hadn't made it. A TIA, or a stroke, but if a TIA, a rather severe one. I called the attendants, who came in, began cleaning her up, and got her into bed. Then I faced a terrible dilemma and (God help me) I chose my professional obligation. I gave the Wyndham Park people my number at Covenant, told them I'd be back in an hour, and went to teach the class. I can't tell you what I said, or whether it was any good. I think it was rotten, and it should have been.

When I got back I sat with her awhile, saw that her blood pressure was too high, and took her by ambulance to emergency and from there to a room at Huntsville Hospital. Most times (nearly every time) she recovers from these on her own, but sometimes not, and how can we tell the difference from the one that will kill her? Still not very responsive when I left her at 6:00. "Okay!" she can say, that's her hole-card word, the last one to go, and "Well, hello!" and "I beg your pardon!" when they ask her something she really doesn't understand. And "I'll be better in the morning," when I tell her that. But having only four verbal output cards to play is pretty close to poverty for that very verbal communicator.

This was the week of Tennessee vacation, which I needed, and Pat needed, for the time with me, even more. Not good news.

But we'll do what we gotta do, no doubt. I'm okay, but tired. It's been a long day.

AUGUST 10, 1992

It's now Monday morning. I'll go to the hospital by 7:00, to be there when Dr. Holdsambeck comes by and to see what the night's rest has done for Betty's recovery. This appears to be of about the same magnitude as the episode in March, when I went to Littlefield to get her out of the hospital. She had that one on Sunday night, and by Wednesday was still moderately wacky. The other two she has had here were quicker recoveries, about twelve hours. I'm not convinced yet that it's a stroke.

And she is such a battler! My word.

I can't stop thinking about the future, trying to make decisions that aren't here yet, for which I don't have all the information I will have when I have to make them. Can she go back to Wyndham Park, and when? With what kind of assistance? Will there be some time in nursing care? Additional precautions? A walker? (Drat, drat!) Permanent damage? Medication for next steps? And, so selfishly, do we get to go to Tennessee this week to the Cumberland Plateau? That's terrible, but it's a real question and, of course, Pat feels it. When we were talking about this last night, I said, "Well, the old gal kept us from leaving town," and Pat said, "She couldn't help it." Not always do we take those mutually supportive approaches.

AUGUST 10, 1992, LATER: *Another Bounce*

Bouncing Betty has bounced back one more time. When I went by at 7:00 this morning, she was alert and speaking English, and feeling normal. The doctor says she's "back to the baseline." Wants to run more tests, since he says the contrast between Sunday's absolute passivity and Monday morning's recovery is just astonishing. He's looking at blood-vessel blockage someplace, however.

So we're vacationing in Huntsville, between hospital visits, and it's okay. At least the phone rings less here. We may still be able to get to Tennessee on Wednesday or Thursday, depending on how long Dr. Holdsambeck wants to keep her in hospital.

August 11, 1992

Mom continues to recover, miraculously. She says she's well, wants to go home, and has used that word to refer to her Huntsville residence more than ever before. Sunday afternoon she was listed in poor condition by the ambulance driver; she could not walk, talk, hear, respond, or anything. One of her four bottom-line verbal responses after she started to recover a little was "I'll be better in the morning," and that must have been the programming language her psyche was using on itself, since she was indeed massively better in the morning. And continues to be so. She is about 95 percent back to where she was before the attack, with a little fumbling for words now and then, but she can fake it wonderfully. She had two pastoral calls yesterday, Henry Pope from Faith Church and Sally Lorey from First in Huntsville, and faked it superbly with both. We came in while Henry was finishing up, and she got in trouble and dropped the ball only when Henry said, "Now you remember what I told you to tell Houston," and she said, "I can remember anything!" He asked her what it was, and she got this stricken look. She had no idea what she was supposed to remember.

Unless the doctor finds some cause for these attacks, she'll go home today. I think she'll be able to function okay back at Wyndham Park, since they provide some extra care for those who are in need. Plus, we'll get to leave for Tennessee either today or tomorrow! Be back Saturday, for a full Sunday and a roaring week ahead.

AUGUST 13, 1992

Betty's still in the hospital. Dr. Morgan, the new neurologist, is concerned about some continuing confusion and memory lapses. He's doing all kinds of tests to see if he can spot any connection between the migraines she's suffered since college and these current attacks. She may be in the hospital through the weekend. So, we're still vacationing in our own condo in beautiful downtown Huntsville, which isn't all that bad, with nice, comfortable bed and bathroom facilities to which I'm thoroughly accustomed. We're eating most meals out so Pat doesn't have to cook, like a vacation, and I'm sleeping, patching stuff, puttering, doing computer catchup, and taking naps between hospital visits. Not so bad, not so bad.

AUGUST 14, 1992: *Living Like Tomorrow*

The last workday of vacation dawns and here we are in Huntsville, with the alluring Crossville, destination of our aborted holiday, a world away on the other side of that hospital room. But we gotta do what we gotta do, and the Cumberland Plateau isn't going to go away, so we'll get there sometime, probably next summer. It will be even better for the wait. I think I am resting, and the phone rings less often, except for those calling to see how my mother is, bless 'em, those who wake me up from my afternoon nap when I'm finally able to not be wrapped up in how Betty is doing. How can I complain? People are good, so good. Janel and Ed Bates sent her a plant, and they hardly know her, but they love *me,* so they showed it that way. Preachers have been visiting. She doesn't remember them from the last time she met them, but she's unfailingly polite and gracious and Bettyesque, so they don't get too offended at not being remembered. So we'll make it.

As I assess the situation, things are not good with my mom. She is in the next phase after where she was before, and I don't know whether this is an early foretaste and she'll come back out or if she will stay there. But this is nursing home behavior. Doesn't know what day it is, what time it is, what's going on. She isn't unhappy, just sits there and nods affirmatively, every so often says, "Okay," and starts sentences she can't finish. "Where are you?" "Hospital." "Which one?" No answer. "What day is today?" No answer. "What time is it?" "Ten o'clock," positively, convincingly, except that it's noon. She fell yesterday trying to get out of bed for some unknown purpose, and has a new cut on her arm. Haven't talked to the doctor today, but it can't be good. What is going to change this? Thank God she's not depressed—doesn't even seem to know that she's confused or disoriented. She has stopped asking when she's going home.

And here we are with vacation over, mom in the hospital with an uncertain future, and a busy fall just around the corner. Mixed news from the front, that's what. Last night Mom seemed a bit better, knew she'd had three roommates while she was there, including the current occupant of the next bed, Mrs. Kim (who could speak no English whatsoever). Betty has recovered enough so that she probably can make it at Wyndham Park in her apartment with some extra help from the staff. I haven't heard from either doctor on Saturday and Sunday; I hope their golf was good. I keep writing different scenarios every time I visit her because her condition changes so much.

August 17, 1992

Dr. Holdsambeck was at the hospital last night when I got there, working late. I repent of the remark about golf. He said my mom was doing well, not poorly, that they'd found nothing to tell when attacks were going to come, and that they could keep her a few more days but had no more tests to run. He thought releasing her was best. She was *so* excited, ready to go back to Wyndham Park. Maybe this will make Wyndham Park more attractive. So I'll go get her this morning.

I still think she's somewhat more confused than before the attack—has more trouble finishing sentences—but maybe part of that could just be the hospitalization and the demeaning, insulting, dehumanizing existence there. She sure perked up when the doctor grilled her, did pretty well on the questions. "Did you have tests today? "Yes." "What kind?" No answer. "Was it surgery?" "No, not surgery!" "Drawing blood?" "No." "Walking?" "Yes, walking." (It was a treadmill test to measure the heart's functioning under stress.)

So we'll try her back at Wyndham Park.

AUGUST 20, 1992: *Back "Home"*

I have the colliewobbles again, the hurting stomach that means I am not in charge and don't know what's next and am afraid. I think I'll play more ocean music. It's Thursday morning, and there are eighteen more hours of care for my mom on the expensive special basis, and then she's on her own again. Can she make it? What will happen? Will she do something crazy? New medicine, is it working? And the clock ticks. I am going to consult a woman in the Regional Council of Governments office, an expert on aging, that my friend Dot recommends. I've got to think about nursing care, as a backup, and the next step when it is necessary.

AUGUST 21, 1992

She is back in Wyndham Park. We've arranged for personal care assistants, eighteen hours a day, mostly just to be with her and keep her safe.

• • •

Back home after an hour and a half with my mom. It was a strange time—a funny "Friday evening visit in her home," while she had a caretaker with her who was like a chaperon. Part of the time she was saner than I am (which is not saying much) and part of the time goofy. She has a pain in her left side. She has no explanation, but winces when she gets up and it hits her wrong. I helped her write two checks, which would pass only at her little West Texas personal bank, where they've cashed her checks for fifty years. Terrible, she couldn't find which line to write on. Sarah, the chaperon, checks out at 11:00. I have a meeting at 10:30 tomorrow, which ends with lunch, then I'll go over. What will I find?

AUGUST 22, 1992

A mostly good day, in that my momma is holding on. Improving every day in verbal recovery, for which I am amazedly grateful. But she has this pain in her side, which acts very much like a broken rib, and I think she did that in the hospital. Also a bad cut on her arm that was very inexpertly treated, so that now she'll have a scar. It should have been stitched, I think, but some attendant who had let her fall evidently bandaged it rather crudely. We'll see Dr. Holdsambeck on Monday, get some tape on her side, and have the arm looked at.

AUGUST 24, 1992

I spent the afternoon getting my mom to Dr. Holdsambeck's. Sure enough, she has a cracked rib. Probably got it in the hospital when she fell. He said the tear on her wrist was badly repaired by someone who didn't want to reveal that she'd fallen and cut her arm on his or her shift. Ah, so. But I doctored it and it's healing now and not infected, though there'll be a scar on that fragile, antique eighty-six-year-old skin. The cracked rib will recover. He told her all she has to do is suffer, and she said she could do that. He asked how her memory is and she said, "Wonderful!" He asked, "Can I ask you those dumb questions?" She said, "Of course." He said, "What day is it?" She quickly and brightly said, "Friday." He responded, "Nope. Monday." He asked "What's your son's birthday?" She said, "Same as it always was." He persisted, "But what is it?" She turned to me, "Tell him, Houston." What an improviser!

OCTOBER 4, 1992

A nice after-church time with mom, who is still in good shape. We went to the Olive Garden and we both had a lot of their wonderful salad and breadsticks. Then she ordered an appetizer-sized serving of stuffed shrimp and that was plenty for her, since servings are usually too large and that bothers her. Then to Baskin-Robbins for a quart of Jamocha Almond Fudge and back to her apartment, where we each had a little dish of that. It is wonderful when things are going well and we can enjoy each other like we did today. I keep hearing the clock ticking in the background, preparatory to another attack (how long, how long? and how severe, how severe? and how many, how many?) She doesn't hear that ticking, or at least gives no evidence of it. Today was sweet.

OCTOBER 8, 1992: *The House is Sold*

It appears that I've sold the Littlefield house. I am filled with great relief and great sadness. I didn't realize the sadness would come, but I should have known that, too. This represents burning a *big* bridge to my past, as well as one of the major connections of my mother with her former life.

She is taking it so well, congratulating me on selling it and getting a good price (which I didn't, of course, considering the current price of real estate in West Texas and the world, and considering the difficulties of handling it from eight hundred miles away.) She has currently determined to smile and optimize and Pollyanna her way through everything, and I like that attitude a *lot,* even though I see the effort beneath her gritty smile much of the time. "How are you today?" "Wonderful!"

So when I told her I had a contract coming in the mail to me, she congratulated me for disposing of the place where she had lived for forty-seven years, where she and my dad were in their prime, where the grandkids came to see her, and where her center for bridge, socializing, church life, and community involvement took place. Burn that bridge—there's nothing behind but the past, nothing ahead but the future. That's the house from which my dad left for the hospital for the last time; that's the one she and I left in May 1992, without a tear. From her, that is.

And, of course, I'm relieved. Winter coming, vacant house in a little West Texas town where the dust was blowing yesterday when I got the word about the sale, yard to mow, gas and electric bills to pay, insurance, decisions about the fence, eaves, and carpet, and everything else. Now there will be some money coming *in* for a change, instead of just going out, out, out. Not as much as I'd hoped, not as much as it's worth, but out from under the burden of it. I translate all of my mom's money into time these days: How many months of Wyndham Park does each transaction buy her? So her wonderful house, the house she and Pop built, the house with (she said) fifty closets, will be traded for two and a half years of Wyndham Park.

JANUARY 18, 1993: *A Little "Spell"*

Betty Hodges had a little spell Sunday. It was not major, but just a little one that flicked out at her brain while we were driving her back to her apartment after lunch. Not bad, but just to show her what it can do when it wants to, and what it will eventually do for good, in time. She started talking sensible sentences, but all out of place. "It'll be hard to do!" she announced. "No time if it will work." No preface, in reference to nothing. Then the litany that tells she's in a spell: "Okay!" she says brightly. "Okay!"

I said, "Mom, do you feel all right?" She echoed, "All right," and the look in her eyes told me she was out of it. She waved her palm in front of her eyes, to show that the vision was blurred. She walked stiffly up to the door, walked past people she knows, got to her room, and sat stiffly in her chair. I helped her take off her shoes, pulled a blanket over her legs, and sat with her. She saw my concern; "I'll all right no matter," she said, "No will okay!" I reassured her, "Yes, I know you'll be all right. After awhile you'll go to sleep, and in the morning you'll be better."

Damn this stuff. I don't know whether it takes what she's proudest of, what she does best, what was added last: her wonderful vocabulary, her analytical mind, her ability to knit and play demon bridge, and her dignity. The sphincter to the bladder goes berserk. The stuff beats her down, attacks frontally, and tries to defeat her.

But it hasn't, yet. "I'll okay!" she said. I left her ready for bed, hoping she'd be fine in the morning.

January 19, 1993

This morning she was better, but still a little goofy: weak voice, hesitant, too long a pause before she answered, the timing gone. "Good morning." "Are you better?" I asked, "Better," she replied, the echo. Then the sign of real recovery, "I think I had a TIA." "Yes, but not a bad one," I told her. "No? Enough, enough!" she responded. Yes, bad enough, indeed.

I went out to see her this morning after breakfast, near 11:00. She was dressed but lying in her bed under the covers, just lying there. I don't think she'd been to breakfast today. I fixed her a cup of coffee and she drank it eagerly. I took her to lunch in the dining room. She poked at food and ate a roll, three bites of pork chop, and all of her sweet potato, and she drank another cup of coffee. Hard to cut the pork chop since she couldn't cut but one direction, so the meat is just sliced, not cut into bites.

Then Betty Hodges, Basic Betty, began to reappear. Mrs. Vaughn was having trouble cutting her chicken with that poor damaged right wrist of hers. Mother looked at her appraisingly, "You're doing well," she said. "Can I help?"

January 24, 1993

What a time! Busy, every minute, with some serious church conflict I'm trying to cope with, and continuing worries about my mom, who lurches from one problem to another. Still some continuing damage showing from her last little TIA, a week ago now: reaching for words, finding the wrong one, and now, a terrible rash on her face.

A pretty good day yesterday, all in all, when I got enough sleep and fought no nightmare the night before. But my mom's face is terribly broken out, quite severe. She hadn't told me, but she hadn't been using her prescription cream, just cold cream. Or shampoo, or who knows what. So I put the prescription ointment on it yesterday morning and reminded her last night to use it. We have a doctor's appointment Monday, and it's got to be better by then or we've got severe problems. It itches and it's hard for her to keep her fingers off of her face. The Assisted Living supervisor called me after lunch to inquire because everyone's concerned. If it's not one thing, it's two more.

FEBRUARY 1, 1993

Once again the Super Bowl is a stinker, but this time at least it's going my way, with the Cowboys way ahead. I'll call my son John after it's over. Looks like it'll be a rout, which will be totally all right with John.

• • •

My mom's not doing well, but she's struggling valiantly. I tried for ten minutes by phone to help her get the volume turned up on her Super Bowl telecast, but couldn't get through to her. She kept reading me players' numbers off the screen when I wanted her to read labels on her TV controller. So she's watching the silent version.

Today there was a wondrous little episode of infinite sadness. I was given a facsimile of an 1837 Huntsville *Democrat,* which happens to include an ad from my ancestor Dr. John Sappington, the quinine entrepreneur. I gave it to her, appropriately circled so she could find it. She read it with amazement, then said, "I have to send copies to all my brothers and sisters." I said, "Mom, the only one left is your sister Rhea, and she's not reading these days." Mom paused, her eyes widened when she realized the truth of that, then she put her head down in her hands. It was the closest to crying she's come in the whole sequence since last year, through the uprooting, the departure from her home, the whole exodus. "My family's nearly gone," she said. "No," I said, "Just those behind you, not those ahead of you. You've got me, and your wonderful grandkids, and little Rachel and Jarred—they're out ahead. That's your family." She nodded silently. It's not the same.

• • •

She was moderately okay at church and at lunch today. She's speaking adequately on automatic and manners stuff, the deep-down, bred-into-the-bone stuff, but not well on current and *ex tempore* stuff. Oh my, what a battle, but she never, never, *never* gives up. God, I only hope I can fight like that when my turn comes. Tough, gentle, little mannerly streetfighter.

Chapter Three

The Intrusion
of Beauty

Prelude

She was always good at adapting and made a virtue of it.
She was 5′4″ and said all the tall boys asked her to dance
because she made them look even taller. My father was two
inches above six feet, but when I was eight, that was a
mountain. Now, however, she faced a taller challenge still:
new state, new apartment, new friends, new church, new
doctor, new hairdresser, new TV schedule, new newspaper,
all of which mattered immensely to her—the landmarks by
which she measured who and where she was today.

Of all the remarkable traits of this remarkable woman,
the most remarkable of all were her unfailing optimism,
her refusal to give up, and her unrelenting ability to cope
with whatever befell her and not be vanquished by it. To
stereotype older folks as acquiescent, unresisting, and com-
pliant is to misread the determination of Betty Hodges.

I think she got this from her girlhood. As the last of six
children of a Cumberland Presbyterian minister's no-frills

family, there was still plenty of food and love and hand-me-down clothes to spoil her. The advantage to being spoiled is that you know forever that you're special and deserve the best. If what comes to you doesn't know it's the best, you may have to change its mind for it.

The three big brothers teased her, protected her, and spoiled her. Two big sisters took her to raise for their very own, like a doll. The father, "The Reverend," was classic absentee, busy meeting every family's needs except his own. Kate, his wife and the classic invalid, sat in her chair on the porch, but she taught the children to sing and how to speak.

When the girls took over raising their little sister, they were eight and ten years older, so they were up and out when cute little Betty was ready to train. Virginia and Ida Rhea were brainy and intense. One summer Gina got jobs for her and Betty at Yellowstone as "savages," to make beds and clean rooms in exchange for free time to roam and savor. Another summer Gina got them both jobs in the New York City library, at different branches. They shared a tiny apartment which they never were at except for sleeping, saw all the plays, and walked to all the tourist attractions. I suspect that Gina liked having bubbly Betty with her for the doors that my mom's smile could open (and the boys it could summon!), to supplement Gina's somewhat formidable intensity, which sometimes put people off.

Ida Rhea was the brilliant intellectual who always knew everything. She gave baby sister an unquenchable curiosity about the universe, no subject too arcane (and if it is, don't admit it). In latter years Rhea joined the Ethical Culture Society, too sophisticated to accept her parents' religion, too much influenced by it to reject it. How did do-gooder get to be a bad word? Betty learned from the cradle that she was here to make the world a better place, spot by benighted spot.

So when the tests of being transplanted to Alabama came, Betty had learned decades before that life was fine, that people were to be trusted, and that there were constant rewards from being good, working hard, and saying nice things about people.

In Betty's new life there were forever pleasant surprises. Just when it looked gloomy, the sunshine appeared. Or she could turn on the light and pretend the sun was coming out. Her Alabama doctor said about her that he was convinced that when people have nothing but good poured into them all their lives, that's what comes out in the closing phases.

One of the most reassuring surprises of caring for the aging is meeting others who are engaged in the same task, who make their living at it, and finding out how compassionate and capable they are. I was worried about this, from the newspaper stories and television exposés of elder abuse. I know there are some who take out their own frustrations on those in their care, and I'm sure there are a few who act out half-buried hostilities against their own parents by mistreating those they're employed to care for. But that has not been my experience, with only one or two exceptions. I'm sure it is important to do the best research one can do to guide the choices of housing, physician, and treatment options, but it's my theory that the vast majority of those involved in elder care are self-selected as caring people themselves. They have to be, to do it.

Since many of the decisions about the lives of your loved ones are so terrible, and so permanent, it's a temptation to make them quickly and even heedlessly, then to put them behind you with relief. Resist this; do the best you can to decide thoughtfully, using the counsel of your siblings. If you're handicapped by being an only child, as I am, you can still consult with friends, and will find many others in the same leaky boat as you. Therefore, ask at your church or club or neighborhood about the plans you're making for the person whose decisions you must make for them. Stop in the parking lot at the residential facility you're considering, and you'll find a relative of someone who's there.

My experience with those who help care for Betty has been very positive. Reasoning tells me that the wages paid for elder-care workers can't be very high. The work is sometimes demanding, unattractive, or discouraging, and sometimes people born in the early decades of the twentieth century show prejudices and demanding impoliteness toward those who provide assistance in their daily living. I've seen more mistreatment of nursing-home staff than of residents! In these five years I've gotten an overwhelming impression of earnest, thoughtful compassion toward the residents of the large retirement complex she moved into, the hospital, the rehabilitation center, and the second, smaller assisted living home.

There are other intrusions of wonder and grace in this life to decorate its gray-tinged walls with bursts of beauty. There will be a conversation, unexpected and at random, where memories of childhood long past come fresh as tomorrow morning to highlight truth. There will be a delightful hour in the mall, or at the beach, or by the side of a hospital bed, when truth and compassion are running high. A visit by a great-grandchild will spotlight nearly a century of a family's life, and put it in bookends. Or through the fog of forgetting will come a crystal-clear word of love and the touch of a beloved, wrinkled hand that floods the room and your heart with light.

It pays to listen, even when you think there is silence, and to wait, even when you don't know what you're waiting for.

In this chapter you'll hear more about the balancing act that's required when you're working hard at something you love, when you're trying hard to care for a beloved person who's always surprising you with emergencies that keep you off-balance. During this time I was planning my retirement from denominational executive service, while I skated on the increasingly thin ice of my mother's situation.

That retirement actually came to pass in April 1995. So, forty-two years of active ministry were wrapped up, passing like a watch in the night.

Then you'll hear a little about the job of interim pastor in Fayetteville, Tennessee, just twenty-five miles north of Huntsville. I took that on as a purportedly half-time job, to keep me from meddling in the affairs of the job from which I'd retired. Half-time, hah! When I want to get tremendous tasks accomplished with one salary, I think I'll hire two half-time beavers, since they have to work about 90 percent of the time to get their internal work quota filled.

I loved the interim work of filling in while a new permanent pastor was sought. There was the retreading of old skills long dormant, discovering new growth areas, and loving the part of the service called Children's Time, all the time keeping a wary eye and ear cocked to the south, where Betty kept her life on hold, waiting for the next episode.

MAY 10, 1993: *Mother's Day in Alabama*

It's still an institution, with people wearing white and red flowers to church. I was very conscious of the sameness and difference from the past. A year ago I was in Littlefield herding my disoriented mom through her last service in her beloved home church, and trying to pack her things, while every time I turned my back she took something out of the box that I'd just packed and put it back in her closet. This year it was Mother's Day in Alabama, against a background of pastoral distraction, the poor condition of my most senior pastor, Ed Dalstrom. I was in Birmingham Friday for the insertion of his second pacemaker. When I left he was doing fine, but at 6:00 P.M. he threw a cardiac arrest at them. They snatched him back with no damage and have him in Cardiac Intensive Care, listed as poor. So I decided not to go to a meeting in North Carolina but to hang around here and, as a bonus, make a little afternoon coffee visit to my mom.

So, our day was fine. Ed Dalstrom's doing okay, I had a good visit with my mom, and she got at least two phone calls from grandkids, John and Chris, so they stay in the will. I went over to Wyndham Park about 2:00 and we just talked, read some letters she'd gotten, drank a cup of coffee, and had a good relaxing time. She wanted to talk about why she couldn't remember things and why she's here, so we did that some. She said, "I do pretty well most of the time, and then sometimes I suddenly get a dump (nice phrase, but that's how she said it) and don't want to be here." "Yep," I said, "I understand. You want to be in Little-field and in your house and able to drive your car and go to your church and see your friends." "Yes," she said. We talked some more about why that isn't possible and how glad I am that she is here. She doesn't remember so many things, like being in the hospital in Lubbock and the one here in August, and how she got around in Littlefield after they took her car away (arch glance at me, she knew who the culprit was). There was nothing about packing or the drive here or moving into Wyndham Park. She shook her head at all she's forgotten, then said with relief and conviction, "But I remember all my friends!" "Yes," I said, "they're deep, deep down in your soul."

DECEMBER 21, 1993: *Christmas Shopping*

Betty Hodges went to the mall today for Christmas shopping. An hour or more, nearly an hour and a half, moving quite slowly, stopping every few feet to look at something new, something bright, something flashy, something neither she nor anyone she knows could use or would wear. But it was there, and she doesn't get to shop much. Stopping at garish teenage fashions to lift the hanger off the rack and look at the skimpy, glittering thing appraisingly, just short of trying it on. To the slippers corner to buy blue slippers for her daughter-in-law; to the candy shop in the center to pick sugar-free candies for her dieting granddaughter-in-law; and then to the men's department to pick an expensive white shirt, the best in the store, for her preacher son. I explained that I'll close my eyes while I wrap it for her.

She rested three times, sitting on the benches in the middle of the mall: "In just a minute I'll be ready to go again."

The last time, I saw her watching the crowd appraisingly, looking intently at each passerby. She saw me watching her, ducked her head apologetically. "I just keep thinking," in that strange town I moved her to, a million miles from home, "that I'll see someone I know." Then she pulled herself to her feet for the rest of the task.

MARCH 4, 1994: *A Call from a Chris*

Let me tell you this week's Betty Hodges story. You know I've got a son Christopher, right? He's job hunting and mom is very concerned about that. She urgently wants him to find work. So when I called her Wednesday night she told me Christopher had gotten a job and moved to Alabama. She went on to say he'd told her about the *Huntsville Times* and they had had a nice conversation. He'd given her his number, 532-4444, but when she called it she hadn't gotten him.

Aha! The "4444," the circulation number of the *Huntsville Times,* twigged with me. That's the only phone number she's remembered in two years, but she got that one down pat. Some guy had called her and said, "This is Christopher." She had immediately asked if he had a job, where he was calling from, all that, and he responded, then talked with her about the *Times* and subscribing thereto. She must have loved that, since anyone who talks about newspapers gets an extended conversation with her. I finally asked if it sounded like her Christopher. She sadly, said "No, it didn't." But she was so glad to be talking with him that she was willing to overlook that.

Well, that's marvelous, and such a story about how her head works these days. I wonder what ol' Christopher at the *Times* is telling about his chat with that funny lady. (She didn't get him because she has to dial 9 before a call and consistently doesn't remember to do that.)

May 4, 1994: *A Date with Paul*

My mom had a date last week. She got an engraved invitation to a prom, tried to explain it to me without much success, until I found the invitation later. She went, nonetheless, wearing her Easter dress, her prettiest outfit. It was Saturday night from 6:00 to 9:00 at Wyndham Park, her apartment building. She later reported that she'd had a date with Paul, who is sixteen, and that they'd danced and danced. He gave her a corsage and, after the dance, asked to escort her to her room. (Wicked Chris Hodges said later, "I hope he was careful!") Turns out to be a service project of a high-school service club, and I think a wonderful idea. She said, "Some of those old ladies could really dance."

All I could do to compete with young Paul was take her to Copeland Sunday morning for dedication of the new building, replacing one damaged by fire fourteen months ago. It was a raging success, with 250 people there in a church that has 75 members. A wonderful service and an even more wonderful dinner on the grounds afterward. Mom shone; she loved the crowd and all the activity and soaked up all the attention (and didn't mind that her son had a prominent liturgical role in all the festivities, which included getting to be in line first to eat).

NOVEMBER 12, 1994: *Two More Sips!*

I've been reflecting some on the next phase for my mother and starting to think about how to manage that, whatever it is. It will be more expensive than the Assisted Living, if she's in Nursing Care, about $2,500 per month. I am hoping she can stay in Assisted Living for as much of her journey as possible, and that she doesn't require all that much Nursing Care, since it will deplete her resources much more quickly. Currently, she doesn't need all that Assisted Living provides, and it is pretty expensive itself, about $1,700 per month for the basic room and board, plus all that goes with that: field trips and transportation to grocery stores, banks, the library, and such. But it sure is nice to have the things that are essential, like safety, nutrition, and socialization. I went by to get her a few Sundays ago and they were redressing her. Two housekeepers had her stood up there like a Barbie doll, taking off her skirt and blouse, which were soiled, and replacing them with others. One of the housekeepers held earrings to Betty's ears appraisingly and said, "Let's put these on you, they look nice," while mom had to stand there and take it. Ah, ah, the loss of independence. With the very best of intentions.

Her weapons are many. One that she's found is "Two more sips," as a magic phrase to keep doing what she enjoys greatly, sitting at the table after a meal to relax before having to go back to that dull apartment. So she savors that last part of the cup of coffee, knowing that it's hard to argue with "Two more sips"—that the housekeepers in her dining room and her impatient son find it hard to counter that with, "Get on your feet and get out of here, you powerless old woman!" So, she uses that as a talisman against the loss of her independence. *That* she can say: "Two more sips!"

I get impatient with her and sometimes she fires back. "What do you want to bawl me out for now?" she asked this week. So I need to balance my criticisms with praise and appreciation for her gallantry and adaptive skills, for how hard she fights against the fog, and for the simple enjoyment of the fun and love she brings to the world. She knows her job is to make the world a better place to live in, and that means Wyndham Park right now. It's a pretty big institution for one little old lady to take on, but by God she does it. She gives advice, solicited or not, tries to help people find their rooms, and puts up with their idiosyncrasies and how self-centered and damaged they are. She doesn't count herself in the category of the damaged or deprived, of course. Or the lost.

DECEMBER 4, 1994: *More Help, Huh?*

The audiologist says there's significant hearing loss with my mom, so much so that her one ear wouldn't benefit from a hearing aid, but that she needs one in the other.

We're thinking about it. It would be a considerable hassle for her to keep up with, changing batteries and such. She has such trouble with her TV already, and she can see the controls for that. So how can she deal with that little dial in her ear? But in church she is missing a lot of what others are saying, and that's very important to her. She was pretty good at the exam, after she tried her first routine of "There's nothing wrong with me." Then he put her in the soundproof room and tested her with different sound levels showing her where she confused words people normally can keep straight. That appeal got to her.

December 14, 1994: *Cards for Another Christmas*

Off this morning for Wyndham Park and taking my mom her Christmas cards. Part of the time she worries that she will have to address all the envelopes, since she "doesn't know where all the addresses are." Wrong: she doesn't know where *any* of the addresses are. The rest of the time she's grateful that I've got them saved on my computer's label program, with only a modicum of resentment about my doing it for her. She's always starred in Christmas cards. But it's okay, we'll get them out.

This will be the day for taking my mom Christmas shopping, just like last year. We'll surprise me with another white shirt, and try to find something as a gift for Pat on which mom can waste her money. We were supposed to go shopping Friday. When I tried and tried to find her by phone, I finally called the desk and they told me she'd left for Opryland in the Wyndham Park van. That's one hundred miles away, in Nashville, and a very demanding (and quite exotic) trip. One hundred miles might just as well be around the world for her. It must have been a rather strange day, but they made it. I feel sure that she was downstairs when they loaded the van and just marched herself onto it and went. She said she didn't want to live there. Me neither.

DECEMBER 26, 1994

We had a good Christmas day, with calls to the scattered progeny. Bruce and Chris were together in Manhattan, where Bruce fixed gumbo. I can report that the various Hodges got money for singing in seven Christmas services in twelve hours: Jim and Susan in Minneapolis for three services, Chris in Philadelphia for two, and John as choir director in Bay City, Texas, for two. The only amateur of the bunch was little Rachel, John and Cindy's five-year-old, who sang her first solo of "Away in a Manger," all three verses, from memory.

Christmas was even a miracle of heavenly peace at our quiet house in Huntsville, despite strain and stress on the international scene, from which our lives are not exempt. Call it the realm of peace, even if on a smaller scale.

I went to get my mom about 9:00 Christmas morning, and she and I built and watched the fire for an hour, good for character building, while Pat got to sleep late. Then, when she got up, we had coffee and presents, turkey sandwiches with pink champagne, and calls to the kids, all successful. The calls were particularly warm and full and loving, and I loved 'em.

DECEMBER 27, 1994

The best thing about Christmas was my new house shoes. My mom and I had gone out Christmas shopping at the mall and had done it well. I'd suggested two presents for Pat, we'd bought them with Mom's credit card, and I'd picked out my surprise shirt; she was pleased. I took the presents home and wrapped them, and they were under the tree. She was going to do the tags when she came over on Christmas Eve, and that was fine.

She showed up Christmas Eve with two ragged presents: an envelope with some recycled Christmas seals on it, taken off of Christmas cards she'd received, and a small bundle wrapped in brown wrapping paper held together with yards of sticky tape, and with no indicator of a To/From tag visible. At the time she said it was for me, both were for me, and that it's hard when you can't go to the store. The card was a sticky-sweet religious Christmas greeting, which she'd edited in scrawly ballpoint by adding and subtracting parts of the message as she needed to. The parcel contained a pair of incredibly cheap Korean house slippers, size eight super-wide, which means made to fit a very short three-hundred-pound midget with EEEE-width feet. Seems that some group came by and let the Wyndham Park people "pick a gift to give, pick a card to send," and she'd gone and done the very best she could. What a kind project by some thoughtful church group, that's point one; point two is that gallant old gal just couldn't not surprise her son with something she'd done.

She made me tell her—I was unkind enough to, but I tell her the truth every time I can—that the size of the shoes wasn't quite right, but the spirit of the gift was magnificent. So she said, "Well, you can exchange them, they're of very fine quality." She was right, of course.

FEBRUARY 27, 1995

My mother has a boyfriend. She has been out twice in the past two days, the first time to lunch at Shoney's (a big-time spender) and the second for Mexican food, and to Kroger's for grocery shopping in his flashy red car. She has decided she really does like red cars, a lot. She almost knows his name, which has an S U R in it someplace. That will really look good on the police report when I tell them about her disappearance: "Some guy in a red car, whose name has S U R in it someplace."

APRIL 26, 1995: *Unwanted Swain*

My mom has been a victim of sexual harassment. She's almost eighty-nine years old, but she doesn't have an exemption certificate. No, it was not by the man in the red car, thank goodness.

She pushed the steak knife across the breakfast table toward me. She always comments that they've extravagantly provided her with a serrated knife rolled up in her breakfast napkin, and I always respond in some way, part of our ritual: "Don't use it." I asked her, "You want to talk about something?" She responded, "I didn't know whether I should," and I knew she wasn't talking about the knife.

"Yes, you should," I told her, and waited for what was to come.

"A man . . ." she was hesitant, "a man . . . approached me, he . . ."

I waited. "He propositioned you?" I tried.

"He bothered me," she finished. "He sat too close to me, and he took my hand, and it wasn't right, I didn't like it."

"Where was this?" I asked. "In the living room," she told me; that means one of the sitting rooms or lounges in the retirement complex where she lives.

"Were there other people there?"

"Yes," she told me, "But they didn't notice what was going on."

"What did you do?" I asked.

She said, "I moved away—I didn't like it—but he moved, too."

We changed the subject. We can't talk about anything ultimately serious for too long a time, and must hope there will be a chance later on to take it up again. There was, after we talked about our cousin Ginger Rogers' death, at so young an age.

"What did the man do after you moved and he moved with you?" I asked.

"It was all right, I rejected him," she said, then hastened to add, "I wasn't tempted at all!"

"Somehow I didn't think you were," I told her. She continued, "He wasn't at all attractive. I'm glad I don't know his name."

"I wish you did," I told her.

She reiterated, "I'm glad I don't." She paused. "I don't know if I should have told you."

"Of course you should have," I said. We changed the subject and left the table. Walking down the hall to her room I took it another step, "He sat too close and took your hand? He didn't say anything?"

"He patted me."

"He patted you?" I confirmed.

She said, "Yes, petted." I hadn't heard that word since 1958, and I knew that she knew what it connoted then. When we got to her room I pushed ahead, "Tell me about the petting. On your bosom?"

"On my . . . rear," she said. "That's what bothered me, it went too far."

"Yes," I said, "It did, if you didn't like it."

"Oh, no!" she said with zeal. "I thought about all those other women like me. I've read about this, they have no resources."

"But you have resources," I told her, "And you are strong and resourceful. If this continues in any way, you'll tell me and we'll do something about it."

It was clear that she was deeply troubled by the experience, needed to reflect upon it and talk about it, just as much as if a twelve-year-old were pushed beyond her limits. The boundaries are just as clear when you're nearly ninety. She knew what she felt, she knew he'd gone beyond what was acceptable, and she knew it was real. "I've had a long, and full, and wonderful life, and this has never happened to me before." "You've been fortunate," I told her. "Yes," she agreed, "so fortunate." As if all that had gone before was preface, she now entered a new phase, the time after she'd been involuntarily taken advantage of. Her will, her precious independence, her own personal integrity had been violated. I understood it again in a new way.

When I was leaving she said again, "I don't know whether I should have told you. I thought about it a lot." I told her, "Of course you should have. I'm glad you did. Thank you for telling me. If it happens again, we'll do something about it. I think I won't do anything this time, in hopes he got the message. Is that all right?" She nodded, "I handled it. I think I can."

"I think you can, too," I told her.

"Thank you for trusting me," she said.

"I do, mama, and I'm glad you are so strong."

July 8, 1995: *The Next Siege*

My mom has been hospitalized for a week with a TIA, and pneumonia as a secondary condition. She came back pretty strongly and was released to a rehab center yesterday for respiratory and physical therapy. I went by today and walked her up and down three halls, which is quite a distance, and she did well. I will go in tomorrow afternoon and (as I told her) take her outside. She hates it, with people screaming and moaning all the time, and she wants to fix them. I told her it was so she would want to get out that much sooner. This place has two kinds of folks in it: those who are dying, including the vegetative, and those in need of some intentional rehabilitation. It's a little hard to distinguish them sometimes, but my mom is clearly in the rehab category, at least as long as she continues to progress.

I hope she'll need only a week or two of this. Her oxygen level is down, 70 percent of normal capacity. Her doctor, who is getting to know her pretty well, told someone she is so good at faking it that you can't always tell she's oxygen deprived. She has a set routine of politically correct "little old lady" comments that she can bring out without thinking, even while her well-used mind is in a total fog "My, it's green here, so green!" She gets caught every so often when she says that in the middle of Antarctica or the Siberian steppes, but it usually works. "There's so much news in the paper, and so much of it is bad!" "The weather is nice, but I suppose it's going to change. But we always need rain."

JULY 1995, LATER

I've canceled initial plans to go to Cincinnati for the General Assembly. Betty Hodges has been battling back from pneumonia. That's tough, at eighty-nine years, but once again she has shown there are many virtues in simple courage. The task of recovery has been made more challenging by a couple of what her doctor calls spells (TIAs) she underwent just before the onset of the pneumonia. They make memory more difficult, put the last word in the sentence just out there beyond reach, and infuse rubber into her leg bones. It must be like going out for the fourteenth round of the title bout with a Halloween mask on your face, cotton in your ears, and spaghetti in your legs.

Try that with the added indignity of being treated like a side of beef, a rather frail side of beef. And wearing those hospital rigs, and trailing an oxygen cart behind her with a hand as purple as a plum, from where the IV had slipped and color-stained her hand with a truly garish bruise. Plus no lipstick. Pretty spectacular.

She's been in the rehab center for four endless days and Does Not Like It. Does not know why she's there, does not like breathing deeply. Wants to take the oxygen tubes out, and tells the young speech therapist that she's been talking very well, thank you, since well before that young woman's *mother* was born, and that she doesn't need *her* corrections, thank you very much. Poor Ina is earning her pay.

But Betty never gives up, never gives up, never gives up. "How long do I have to stay here, and when can I get out?"

Wednesday her doctor said her oxygen level was up and climbing, her strength was good, and her walking steady, and that she was trying to take over the management of the place.

I told her today that Dr. H. said he could probably release her Monday, for return to her assisted living apartment. Wow, has that place changed in her perspective, from a somewhat boring facility where she doesn't get to raise much hell because all there is is a bunch of old people to a highly desirable resort. Yes, yes!

I also told her that, if all continued to go well, I might head to Cincinnati on Tuesday to catch the second half of the General Assembly. She said, "Good, you'll like it." Then, "Do you need a new suit?" "I have a new suit," I told her. "Do you need any shirts?" "I have some, honey," I told her, "like the nice white-on-white you gave me for Christmas." "Good," she said authoritatively. "You'll have a good time."

Back in charge.

JULY 17, 1995

We're doing all right. I'm sweating out my mom's recovery, watching the enormous struggle she undergoes *every day* to return to herself. She's been very aware this time that "I'm not myself." She has said that frequently and doesn't like it. Works to remember, to breathe deeply, to walk, to remember to go to the bathroom. It's working, this time. Her doctor calls her feisty, and she really is. I watched her take apart her speech therapist Friday, and the poor woman had to retreat to sheer authority: "Because I can help you, because I went to school and learned how to help you." Trying to get her to tell what town the rehab center was in: "Same as it always was." "Yes." "Alabama, that's it." "Well, Alabama is close enough." When the therapist said, "Huntsville," mom said, "Of course! Glad you remembered."

I've also been enjoying some downtime that I was supposed to be using in Cincinnati at the General Assembly. I'll go up late Monday or early Tuesday and be there for the busiest part, even though it would be very helpful to have been there during the committee meeting time. That's when you can discern what's really going on more easily, poking around in the halls, talking to people in the coffee shops, tracking down rumors. By the time I get there it will be time for the big plenary sessions. I can still see folks I dearly love and get close to the center of the change happening in this church that means so much to me.

• • •

Betty's supposed to be ready to check out of Hillhaven and for me to take her back to Wyndham Park. Doctor has ordered some home-health people to come in for five days to provide extra care during the transition, and that's good.

JULY 28, 1995

Gosh, what happened to all that time I used to have before I retired?

As I pointed out to the Fayetteville flock a long time ago—maybe three weeks—these days I craftily divide each week into two short weeks. There's a little teeny week as the energetic, bustling, hard-charging rookie interim pastor in Fayetteville, from Saturday night through Tuesday night. Then comes a little teeny week as the relaxed, retired putterer and naptaker in Huntsville, from Wednesday morning through Saturday afternoon. At the church door that day, Patrick Tice, who is about six years old, showed that he got it: "Have a nice two weeks!" he told me cheerily.

I stay in the sparsely furnished manse in Fayetteville like a confounded monk: my TV schedule, my bathroom, my bathroom to clean, my meal schedule, my kitchen to clean, my bedtime, my bed to make. I can watch the Braves or access PresbyNet (the computer communication network) or work on sermons with the PowerBook or be lonely any way I please. How do priests take it, year after year, and no wonder they get so much done.

During my Huntsville miniweek I stay in our lavishly appointed condo like a bloomin' potentate, unable to pick my TV programs unless I go upstairs, always taking out the trash or having to go through a pile of junk or bringing my laundry down to the utility room or some other manifestation of being loved intensely. How do ministers' spouses make it, year after year, with the blasted monomaniacal people they live with, the Crazed by God?

• • •

Well, if you pack two extra weeks into each of the last two weeks, it got really hairy. The most important of the extra weeks was the care for my zany old mother, who's back in her apartment and much gladder to be there than before, when I remind her of how much she disliked the rehab center. She seems to have slipped a knot down the rope since the attack that hospitalized her, and now her doctor prescribes oxygen all the time she's in her room. A powerful little puffer-gadget sits there and distills oxygen out of air and tubes it to her. It helps her remember better and talk more clearly. When she doesn't use it, she gets so she doesn't know she needs it. And that's a problem. We're trying to learn together.

• • •

The fourth week that week was called Cincinnati and the two-hundred-seventh Presbyterian General Assembly. I did that in four days, which is really compacting it. I got my mom paroled from rehab Monday morning, left at noon for the drive north, spent the night in Louisville, then made the summit dash early Tuesday. By 10:00 I was interviewing people in the Convention Center. My job this year was to be staff essayist for the communications office. They paid my way, and in return I got to float, flit, hear, delve, sift, smile, muse and write. I do my writing on the lovely little Macintosh laptop, then yoke it to a phone line and upload the result to the Louisville computer that's waiting to store it and deliver it to others when they ask. If anyone does.

I had this terrible compulsion to play catch-up. I'd originally planned to be there Friday, and not arriving until Tuesday morning put me several bricks short of the Pharaoh's quota (the Pharaoh into whom I turn God from time to time.) So I had to hustle to get at it. The easiest thing I could think of on the eight-hour drive there was to analyze my own feelings and see if others had them, too: What's it like to get there dumb, early *or* late, and have to turn that into capable? So I decided to interview first-year commissioners, those who'd never been to a previous assembly, to ask them how it felt and, especially, how it felt to be there from Saturday to Tuesday—the four days I'd missed—and what factors worked on them to help them feel competent.

So that's what I worked on first. While I was at it, I decided I'd interview other folks to ask how they felt about electing our remarkable new moderator, Marj Carpenter, and what her election means for our church. I knew that everyone would have an opinion about that one, and all I'd have to do is stop them in the hall, ask them my question, and prepare to capture their effusive reply. Pick a couple of easy subjects, get them done, get the stories online on PresbyNet, and start listening for what else is going on.

So that's how my career as Boy Essayist began. By Tuesday afternoon I found a phone jack I could link to the PowerBook and uploaded the first two stories. I wasn't particularly proud of them, but thank goodness I got enough positive feedback to show that some folks identified with them.

The rest of the assembly is something of a blur. Eighteen or a hundred committees kept meeting off down a hall somewhere. The ones I picked to watch were paralyzing, while the real action was taking place a mile away. It was like choosing a line at the bank or the grocery store. Then plenary started—that grind guaranteed to substitute for a lobotomy in changing commissioners' personalities. Three nonstop days of too much paper, too little time to read it, people haranguing you that you don't understand, being forced to make decisions you're not competent to make on the basis of too little information, and some of that spurious. You also have to watch the clock while you do it, because you're supposed to be three lines farther down in the docket. This, the Presbyterians claim, is how the voice of God comes through to us these days.

Chapter Four

Nibbling Away

Prelude

This whole thing has been an exercise in subtraction, or better, distillation. Life is ups and downs, a process of gaining, then losing, skills and abilities. Generally the process of aging reverses the gains of infancy and childhood just as they were attained, one fraction at a time, until, at some discrete moment in history, the whole slows down to a crawl of infant helplessness. All that's left is what began, a smile and a breath, and then that leaves and all is still.

With Betty's condition the subtraction has been in phases, usually connected with one of her TIAs, and sometimes with hospitalization. She loses strength and skill and the ability to think clearly. Her speech and mobility are affected, and she is less able than when she started. Her doctor and the therapists who have worked with her are sometimes more optimistic than I have been, but then they've worked with more people like Betty and know how much progress they can make, with patience and diligence and with her incredible determination as a given.

Each new onslaught on humanity is important, because there is a test at the end of it: Is this person still eligible for a certain type of residential care? Can she still walk? Can he take his medication reliably? Can he pay his bills, dress himself, and keep his clothes clean? Can she eat on her own, or does she need assistance? What will she eat if she's left to her own devices, and how long can you live on tea and toast, anyway? Thus, the process of simplification of a human being takes place. What once was complex, a unique interactive construct of all the experiences of life, has now been simpled down to more basic levels of eating, sleeping, breathing, talking, and taking in and emitting the stuff of life.

I took Betty's decline as a personal affront to her and never came to armistice with it. I probably also took it as a distant early warning of what might be ahead for me, since there seems to be a family history of losing it late in life. When a nineteen-year-old attendant was brushing Betty's teeth or trying to get her to speak, I remembered that same Betty giving a speech before one hundred women at a meeting of the presbyterial society. She was alert, vibrant, funny, sincere, and had a special kind of unique tag or hook to make each presentation memorable. I still have her notes on "Knitting in the Bible," in which she told how Palestinian clothes were (and are) made and taught her hearers the Hebrew word for knitting. As the notes indicate, she had gained a little of that knowledge from her seminary-trained son, but once that bit of information was sluiced through Betty's personality, it was hers to share with her listeners.

Now I saw the woman in the bed, unresistant to the treatment being applied to her mouth, and I remembered the Bible speaker. It always made me angry.

The stuff seemed to get the best features of my mother, or at least those abilities of which she was most proud. Perhaps that is the spiritual message of it, which I have not yet comprehended, that the sources of the greatest pride are the abilities to be withdrawn. The ability to speak to groups, articulate, and totally without self-consciousness; the skill as a shark of a duplicate bridge player; the need to devour a daily newspaper or two, page one to the classifieds; good taste in clothes; an unshakable pride verging on arrogance, which I called a family trait passed down from her cultured, elegant, well-bred, ladylike mother—these were what left in her distillation.

Each new day brought assessment with the sunrise. Waken and see what you can do, find out if you can get up, find out if you can get dressed, try to speak, discover if the world looks sensible and you can remember yourself into today, or find out there's been delay, decay, decline, diminution, and work out some new coping strategy to compensate. With enormous creativity, irrepressible determination, and heroic amounts of hard work, one can compensate for anything. Or so that was the claim.

AUGUST 28, 1995: *Change in Climate*

I've told you about the two weeks every week that make my leisurely retirement decidedly unleisurely. I added two more weeks this week, and do not want to do that again.

I had Fayetteville early, as usual, Sunday to Tuesday, then the Huntsville lull. Then I planned to drive to Chattanooga on Friday to do a gig at the East Tennessee Presbytery leadership school, hear Marj Carpenter, and be a big shot. Why can't I learn how dangerous that kind of thinking is, and how I get my comeuppance from the Big Comeupper more often than not?

They woke me at 3:15 last Monday morning in Fayetteville with news that my mom was sitting in her chair in Huntsville saying, "Not good." That's all she could say. I drove from Fayetteville to Huntsville in record time (it's easier at 3:30 in the morning), got her, poured her limp body into some clothes, and took her to the ER of Huntsville Hospital. She'd clearly had another cerebral occurrence of some sort. She recovered some by dawn, so I took her back to Wyndham Park. As soon as I left she fell and bruised her hip. (Why didn't she break the hip? Who knows? Rather, God knows.) I got sitters for her, then took her back to the hospital Wednesday for an MRI and blood tests.

Her wonderful doctor called to say he'd brought in a neurologist to help interpret, but that the scan showed some new stroke-like damage in the brain. Locomotion hesitant, speech impaired, very weak. So with no treatment to give, the hospital was discharging her by Friday. I couldn't find sitters because of the weekend, Wyndham Park wouldn't take her back without sitters, and I was due to leave for Chattanooga at 6:00 that evening. All three sitter agencies promised to try, but none could promise help. Sitters are a rather precious and short-term strategy. Multiply twenty hours by $7.95 an hour, and then try that by thirty days. I could not picture her living in the Wyndham Park environment much longer, with her new limitations.

The divine rescue was through two women who have started a small (3 people) assisted living residence out of their home, licensed and all, which the social worker at the hospital mentioned. I called and either fell in love at first sound or was absolutely desperate, so mom is there for a one-week try at Living Waters, ironically the same name as that of our synod. When I asked Mrs. Dock, the co-owner, where the name came from, she said, "My husband and I were reading the Scriptures looking for the right name, and that one showed up." This mother and daughter team up and started a care facility in their home, got it state licensed, and now have one little old man and two little old ladies, including one somewhat shaky and slightly disoriented Betty Hodges, as residents.

Though disoriented, Betty is politely negative, but at least polite. When I was leaving Friday for Chattanooga, she said, in Mrs. Dock's presence, "You're not going to dump me here?" I had to equivocate and stutter and stammer and dump her there. But she is working at improving, one more time. When I saw her today she was walking better and talking better. Her vocabulary had been working like the WordPerfect spellchecker, so that if it didn't come up with the right word, she dredged up the word next to it in the bin, a "sound-like." But today it was better.

She's lost some ground, but is struggling valiantly to come back, as always. I'm currently renting two care facilities for this next month, the Wyndham Park apartment and the new place, while we decide what's next.

The cute story is that she reads road signs and billboards when she's in the car. So when I was taking her to emergency on Monday in the middle of the night, she was stretched out on the seat, nearly out of it, close to the bottom, not able to sit up straight, absolutely zonked, and I heard her say in the awful still of the darkness, "Not good." And then "Shoney's."

I got to Chattanooga, did my stint with the leadership school and was too tired to be a big shot, drove to Fayetteville Saturday after the school, and preached adequately Sunday. I think I did. I'm not sure I was there, but some of my people said it was okay, God bless them. Sometimes the flock does more than the shepherd.

September 9, 1995: *Lime Green Cast*

Here I am in Minneapolis, thanks to Mickey Miller, Loletia Dock and Lockietee Carter, and Pat Hodges on her lime green cast.

Mickey Miller is a Nashville lawyer, trained in theology, and an architect of the current renewal being carried out in Middle Tennessee Presbytery. He's preaching for me in Fayetteville tomorrow and is one of the parish favorites, so they'll be well cared for.

Mrs. Dock and Mrs. Carter are the two valiant women who've started the Living Waters Assisted Living home, where my mom is. She's been working gallantly (as always) at recovery, is mounting a new and gigantic campaign against the fog that besieges that marvelous mind, and is doing pretty well, though she'll not return to the level of capability she had three weeks ago. But the Dock-Carter team, daughter and mother, may be able to keep her for the next leg of her Journey to Glory. We'll decide together next Wednesday when I get back. But for now she's fine.

And Pat on her lime green cast? Well, that has to do with last Sunday afternoon and our stroll down the sidewalk in front of the manse in Fayetteville. I heard this terrible "thwock" behind me and turned to see my beloved lying flat on the sidewalk. She had turned her ankle on an acorn and fallen, ker-splat. The sound was like a melon hitting the pavement, and I was terrified. She was more worried about torn hose and a bruised knee until she tried to get up and saw the knot on the outside of her left foot, a strange little protruding knot. "It's broken," she said. She's seldom wrong.

We spent the rest of the afternoon in the ER of Huntsville Hospital, slower-paced than the one on TV. Here you wait a lot longer. Young Dr. Swan, who'd treated my mother ten days earlier (and remembered her, of course), looked at the X ray and confirmed the assessment, "It's broken."

No orthopod available on Labor Day Sunday afternoon, unless your arm hung broken with compound fractures, so they wrapped her foot and sent us home. "Do you have crutches at home?" Pat looked at the nurse as if she were bonkers. "No!" she snorted, not in her well-managed home. She will now.

On crutches you get a very quick course in how many things you need both hands for, how many things you can't reach with just one arm when one foot is pinned flat to the floor, how long it takes to get around when you have those two ungainly props to manage, how you have to calculate the size of every opening you traverse. But we made it, and by Tuesday morning I was even more saintly than ever, after playing fetch-and-carry all day Monday. Pat was in misery, foot propped high, trying to sleep on her back, with a twinge at every movement.

Tuesday was a trip to Sports Medicine, along with all the younger people who'd spent Labor Day breaking their pitching hands and sliding legs. She didn't get a choice of white: "What color cast—blue, green, red, or purple?" Mentally surveying her wardrobe, she chose green, and a few minutes later was equipped with the lime green cast. Four weeks, with luck.

She insisted that I go on my long-planned trip to Minneapolis, since it includes before-and-after visits with my daughter Susan and her husband, Jim, outside of Minneapolis. I'm here consulting with the Presbyterian Print Journalism Partnership, the best communicators in the Presbyterian Church, and all I have to do is help them improve their communication.

Thank you, Mickey Miller. And Mrs. Dock and Mrs. Carter. And, of course, dear Pat, with the lime green cast.

September 16, 1995

My gallant momma continues to struggle to improve, so she can stay at the small assisted living home that took her on an emergency basis two weeks ago. She wants to go home, and that means to Littlefield, Texas. But when I told her she couldn't, she said, "Since you explain it so persuasively, I will not contend." I wish she could be in Littlefield, too—that part of the past where her church, friends, hairdresser, police force, florist, grocery store, and neighbors were. All of whom were co-opted to provide part of the safety net that allowed her to live there probably eighteen months after she could not make it on her own.

We were talking about Littlefield this week. I said, "You really miss it, don't you, Momma?" She reflected a moment, then said, "Yes." She paused just a moment longer to calculate, wearing her circle of years like a crown, then said modestly, "I ran it."

She looked at me quizzically. "Didn't I?" I paused in turn before I responded: "Maybe you did, darling, maybe you did."

SEPTEMBER 21, 1995: *Keeping It Going*

I'm back in Huntsville, after an exotic trip to O'Neill, Ewing, Lexington, and Beaver City, Nebraska. I know jealousy is springing up in readers' hearts, just because you drew Palm Springs, Cannes, Fiji, and Rio, while I got Beaver City. It was great, and I learned the difference between angora and mohair. I was also working: leading a workshop, which was fun, for Central Nebraska Presbytery.

There's nothing to make your spouse more glad to see you come home than leaving him or her on crutches. After only eight years in our condo I have finally learned to operate the washer and dryer, and they are very complicated. I don't know how all those clothes were cleaned for the past eight years. Must have been magic. While I was away, Pat survived on food from the freezer and shelves low enough to reach from her crutches, so she was glad to have me back to outsource some of our meals.

I've got three days set aside for eating lunch with my mom, packing up on her apartment at Wyndham Park, learning to operate the vacuum cleaner and the toilet brush at home, finishing the Fayetteville sermon, and unwinding. And being very nice to Pat.

September 22, 1995

Among the six things I was supposed to be about, I had a delightful lunch with my mom, who continues to claw her way back from a time of chaos and deep forgetfulness. On other occasions she's been Bouncing Betty, and has come back with measurable strides. This time the pit was deeper, the darkness darker, and her recovery slower, more irregular. Her doctor says the MRI picture shows that she'll not recover to the same level as before. Therefore, the new place she's living at provides a level of extra care that's now needed.

Today she showed, from time to time, some moments of remarkable clarity, memory of events long past, and wacky humor. Once she said, "I appreciate the time you spend with me." I responded, on a whim, "Glad to do it. It's only fair, since you spent a lot of time on me when I was a kid, that now I can spend some time on you when you're a kid." She grinned immediately, then threw back her head in frank appreciation of the ridiculous role reversal. She laughed with delight.

Then a blockbuster, totally without prelude. She looked at me over her Wendy's grilled chicken salad: "Do you know what?" I asked, as programmed, "What?" She finished the move: "Sometimes I don't know what."

I laughed as she did, in admiration at the completion of the one-two. Then she nailed it down with another, the second verse of the same song: "But I remember that I can't remember."

Ah, Professor Descartes, take that, with your "I think, so I am." This waif with the scarred brain has just replicated your feat: the consciousness of consciousness, awareness of awareness.

I don't know how the minds of cats work, or those of alligators, or those of the coral life forms of the Great Barrier Reef, but I don't think they work like that. I think, in my hubris, that we're the only ones whose minds can make that move, can perform that magnificent trick of sleight of mind—to think about thinking. I was privileged to see it, between bites of a grilled chicken salad.

OCTOBER 7, 1995: *The Circle Narrows*

Her horizon is narrowing and the circles that surround her are getting smaller. That is in preparation for the time, in God's good time, when the circle will be so small (so large!) that it contains only her and God. Then it will not matter if anyone else believes she's breathing or thinking or anything else.

Ten years ago, or fifteen, the horizon was the world she traveled with her buddies. "Where shall we go this spring?

Who's got a new brochure? If we've been there, forget it!"
Beautiful Americans, the purple-haired gang abroad.

Then, after that, the horizon was her little town, the support network that kept her going: her church, her bank, her beauty shop, and above all, her friends. When she had that bad reaction to the codeine cough syrup and drove around West Texas all night long, it was the checker at the grocery store who alerted her friends: "I saw her drive out of the parking lot in the wrong direction and knew she wasn't going home." When her best friend called to tell me, she said, "We've lost Betty!" I thought it meant she was dead. But Susan Wilemon is more literal than that: the Betty-care network had, indeed, temporarily broken down, and they'd simply lost Betty. (They found her again, come dawn, when she drove into her own driveway after escaping a mesh of local cops, state police, and sheriff's deputies, all on watch. They tracked her journey, later, by using the gas-station receipts from where she'd stopped four or five times that night for two gallons of gas and to use the rest room.)

The circle narrowed more down to her house. She kept it as long as she could, holed up inside because it was safe, venturing out only when she had to, to the grocery store and church. They once saw her heading for the grocery store two blocks away, walking at twilight smack dab in the center of the street.

It was then that I moved her, turned her into an involuntary Alabamian, took her to church on Mother's Day, and came back to her house and started packing. We drove to Alabama in May 1992, and the horizon narrowed to someone else's apartment, to someone's caregiving—that troop of anonymous housekeepers who come and go at residences for seniors. Despite all the PR about services and amenities and social activities, it's still a place where you do what they tell you, get up when they say, come to the dining room during their hours or not eat, and get into your lonely bed when they say. Then there is disruption, displacement, the accidents of blood flow in the brain, uncertainty, dislocation—all awry. Hospital, rehab, sitters, being shackled to an oxygen tank, breathing exercises, walking exercises, taking orders, doing what they tell you, telling them who the president is and what year it is (within twenty, and that ought to be good enough)—working, working, working to get back.

Then a new place. Kinder, gentler, smaller, just a few people. Two nice women to give you orders, another woman to share your bedroom, a friendly man who lives there, too: Living Waters Assisted Living Residence. New place, nothing old, nothing of your own but a few photographs: your mother and father, that sweet man who was your everything until he died so long ago, the son, the four treasures who are your grandkids, the two little ones of Generation Five, so strange and so unknown, who are they?

"Where is this? I'm getting along fine. I like it here. I'm doing all right. I want to go home. Is this the place I live?" I took her chair to her when I closed up the apartment. Everything else I dispatched as intended: the two good Heywood-Wakefield pieces to Bruce in New York, the chest to Susan and Jim in Minneapolis since it matches the rest of the bedroom suite they're using, the étagère to our place for display of Chris's origami animals, and a lot of stuff to the Salvation Army. But the chair, a nice recliner, over to Living Waters, to move it into the bedroom.

It was a day or so later when she mentioned it—not a word about where it came from, no curiosity about the rest of the stuff. We had not yet talked about the close of her apartment because I hadn't had courage enough to find the words. But when I called, "I want to thank you for the chair! It's so nice! It makes me feel so good! It's mine." "Yes, mom, it's yours. I thought you'd like it, because it's yours."

The chair and the clothes, on one long closet rod, that's all the room. The photographs and a couple of rubber-banded stacks of correspondence—precious letters and Christmas cards from the past, through which she shuffles time and again to see those beloved names and to read the precious words of care, of small-town news, and of people who remember her. The mirror, with its mottled green back, a 1928 graduation present from her big sister. A little jewelry, mostly junk; the good stuff saved by her son to make sure the future generations get it as intended.

And the chair. The circle narrows.

DECEMBER 12, 1995: *Visitor from the Future*

Bruce Hodges flew in this weekend on a fleeting, fleeing, flying jaunt to see his grandmother: $135 round trip from New York to Nashville. I easily tricked him into letting me drive him to and from the airport, hot dawgie. Two wonderful, captive-audience hours each way, even if the one this morning was just a bit on the early side. Okay, so I got up at 4:30.

The kids are wonderful with their grandmother and I'm glad they know she's on this precarious plateau. None of us knows how long she'll hold there.

When she saw him she clung to him as if not to let him go, as if to pull herself into him. Then she said, "When you come see me, I feel like someone."

In the car she was poking and pounding at my arm and shoulder. She'd pounded him the same way, so I told her, "You like to pound on me because I'm real, because I'm solid. You can touch me good and prove that I'm here." "Yes," she said, surprised that I knew.

DECEMBER 21, 1995: *Insight*

Betty Hodges at lunch December 20: "I think I'm doing remarkably well, considering that nothing works."

MAY 8, 1996: *What's Church?*

Betty Hodges and I went to church Sunday. We picked a small but stalwart parish where she's well known, and they filled her up with greetings and hugs. It doesn't matter so much that you can't remember their names, all that matters is that they say, "It's so good to see you!" and "We've missed you, Betty!"

She was wearing the white suit with a linen look, the white blouse, faux pearls à la the Jackie Kennedy photo, and the white shoes; she was a knockout. Knew it, too, of course.

She said, "Aren't we lucky, it's communion!" when she saw the table. What a greeting to the Lord, winsomely hosting His table.

After church and another raft of farewell greetings by persons who obviously value her and think she's special and needed and appreciated, we settled in the car to go to lunch. She said it reflectively: "That was wonderful church. If it's the last time I ever get to go, it was wonderful."

A month short of ninety gives one a certain valuable perspective.

MAY 25, 1996: *White House Greeting*

She got a birthday card from the White House on Friday and said, "I never got a card from the White House before." First one in ninety years, but it was about time.

You can request one, a month ahead of time, for high-numbered birthdays, by writing to the Greeting Office of the White House. It arrived a week and a day early in an understated white envelope with discreet blue lettering:

THE WHITE HOUSE
WASHINGTON

Her address was written in longhand. Ah, there's a job for a bevy of volunteers eager to help their president and their party: sending out a million birthday cards. Inside, topped by the gold presidential seal, there was a pleasant generic greeting, "our best wishes for a year of good health filled with every happiness" and the two printed signatures at the bottom.

She was really impressed, and the two women who care for her were considerably more so. I was, too. From a busy bureaucracy amid a violent election battle in a nation with more problems than dollar bills, a personal kindness to one of its citizens who's ninety next Saturday.

MAY 31, 1996: *Birthday beyond Politics*

Mom was pleased by the card from the Clintons, though she'd never acknowledge voting for him. My own dear mother went crazy, along with half of West Texas, and fell for a general nicknamed Ike. That opened the door for her and the remainder of the purple-haired gang to vote for Goldwater, Nixon, Reagan, and Bush in turn, and she'll do it for Dole if I drive her to the polling place. But she was very pleased to have the card from the Clintons, as I would have been to have her get one from the Bushes or the Doles. There are some things that transcend partisan politics.

JUNE 12, 1996

Yesterday was one of those days when the talking machinery was not working well. Some days it's pretty good, but yesterday it was labored, sputtering, inconsistent. She'd reach for a word and it wouldn't be there, so she'd have to settle for the one nearby, something close.

There was something she was trying to tell me.

"I want to talk . . . talk about . . . the thing."

"Okay, mom, what thing?"

". . . the . . . you know, that . . . *thing.*"

"No, I don't know. Sorry. Try again."

A long pause; she read a billboard perfectly to test the machinery, which worked fine. Another try: "I saw the . . . the . . . there it was, the . . .," but it wouldn't come.

We drove another minute or two. I could feel the effort in her, beside me. Then very deliberately, each word chosen with care, each one practiced in her head to see that she had it straight, with fierce and singleminded determination: "I haven't . . . done . . . justice . . . to *Monday Morning.*"

Of course! That's the magazine I'm going to edit in my retirement mode, to keep me off the streets. Her own personal copy had arrived Monday (appropriately). Hers had been the first subscription I sent in after I took the job, just ahead of the four for the Hodges kids. It takes time for those to work through the system, but I knew her copy had arrived. She read it as she reads everything from road signs to labels on cans to the daily paper, which she monopolizes as soon as it hits the porch. She brings church bulletins home to read them again during the week, pleasing church secretaries whose weekly labors have never been so appreciated before. Some parts of the mechanism have nearly shut down or are in dire need of repair, but the reading is still there, and that old proofreader's eye is still sharp and demanding.

I said, "Oh, that's all right, Mom. Gee, I've hardly started yet. That issue is not even one I worked on."

She went on, the same fierce and relentless drive: "It's good. I'm proud of you."

Only a mother's love, giving me credit when I don't even deserve it (yet). A mother's love, relentless, limitless, endless, coming through everything, even the boundless fog that hovers right outside her consciousness. I'm pretty lucky.

JULY 18, 1996: *Time Out*

I went by for the weekly outing with my mom yesterday and had to tell her I was going to be doing some traveling in the near future, so I wouldn't be able to see her as often. I explained that Pat and I are planning to run and play in Montgomery this weekend, seeing three plays at the Alabama Shakespeare Festival Theater: "Romeo and Juliet" on Friday night and matinees of "Ladies of the Camellias" on Saturday and "A Winter's Tale" on Sunday.

Then, I explained, the next Wednesday I take off for Montreat, in the mountains of North Carolina, for my stint at the Montreat Youth Conference. There will be two sets of five sermons, each set for a different group of twelve hundred teenagers. I tried to tell her about the mixture of apprehension and divinely insane eagerness with which I was seeing this, the dangers of doing it wrong, and the enormous benefits of doing it right, the natural and supernatural nervousness I was feeling.

She would have none of that. "You'll enjoy it?" I confessed I was hoping to. "You'll do it well." I acknowledged that was my intent, with all my heart. Then, without a pause, she moved on to her involvement and investment in the process, the way she's been doing it for half a century.

"Are your clothes all right?" she asked. Now, what that meant was did I need a new white shirt for the trip. Every Christmas since I've been preaching there has been a new white shirt for the preacher: a history of haberdashery in those shirts, always the latest. We'd moved from nylon and rayon and Orlon and cotton blends to oxford cloth, stopping just short of spandex. More recently she'd done the stylish white-on-white, french cuffs, button-downs—the whole gamut. There has even been an occasional, "far out" one of bluish hue, when those came in style for clergy garb. Even more recently, the sizes have begun to vary somewhat, as she has lost the precise understanding of how her boy differs in build from, say, Wilt Chamberlain or Eddie Arcaro. I still purchase the shirt on her behalf and wrap it not as well as she could and let her sign the card: "Surprise, from Santa!"

So that's what that meant. "I want to support you in what you're going to be doing, in every way I can." The way she asked was, "Are your clothes all right?"

Yeah, mom, I'm okay for shirts. But thank you!

July 23, 1996: *"And in This Corner . . ."*

Betty continues to prepare me for the big job at Montreat, where I'll be living for the next seventeen days. I took her out for coffee today, reminding her that I'm leaving tomorrow, will be gone for some time, but will call every day. Last week she'd checked on my attire, this time it was more basic.

She mused a moment, then asked, "Do your glasses fit all right?" "Yes, mom," I told her, "Eyes are in good shape."

"How about your teeth?" "My teeth fit fine!" I remonstrated. She liked that and laughed aloud, "I mean are they all right?" I reassured her, "Yep, they're fine. I was at Dr. Tucker's a couple of months ago and will go back before Christmas. They're fine."

She switched the subject instantly, checking to see if I was upset with her: "Isn't it remarkable," she asked with assurance, "that we get along with each other so well?" "Yes, it is," I reassured her.

So I think we're ready, and she's done what she can. This is important, after all. It's her reputation that's on the line in the Evening Circle of the Presbyterian Women of Littlefield, Texas, and I just happen to be the one that's carrying out the intentions of that iron will. Montreat, here we come.

I'll call every day, a call to my beloved Pat and a call to my mom. It's a challenge to manage the time difference, to find a pay phone that isn't busy, and to remember to do it, but it's a way of staying sane, remembering where I'm rooted, and keeping perspective.

NOVEMBER 24, 1996: *What's Church For?, Second Verse*

Betty Hodges continues to experiment with the question, "What is going to church, anyhow?" How little of it do you have to receive in order for it to count? We went to Trinity Church again this morning, where people know her and greet her effusively. This was big Thanksgiving lunch Sunday, but we couldn't stay since the wonderful food might have given her the hiccups, which are eventually going to kill her. Of all the dire diseases, including some quite sophisticated varieties you read about in the medical columns, she is most in danger from the simple hiccups, since they lead to coughing, which leads to choking, and a single inhalation can bring the stuff into her lungs that causes aspiration pneumonia. But there was church, and it was world class.

She can hardly hear any of it, so she tends to talk a bit while they're warming up, before the visual display up front becomes lively and fills the screen. She pores over the bulletin intently, until she finds a sentence that's worth absorbing in its fullness. This time she found one buried on the back, which said, "This church is a community of persons who believe in Jesus Christ as our Savior and Lord." She pointed at it, tracing the words slowly, and nudged my shoulder: "I like that," she said.

I glanced at it hurriedly and agreed. She was the second person in all of time to read that sentence. No, the third, first the pastor, who wrote it, then the secretary who replicated it, and then Betty. But it filled her need.

The service proceeded, with considerable variety and not a little modest Calvinistic panoply from the choir, the pastor, the fine organist, an earnest elder with the two little boys for children's time, and the young woman from the children's home during sermon time, telling graphically and quite persuasively of the incredible lives of some of those children flung off by the whirl of today.

Betty heard none of that, I think. She follows along in the hymn book with her eyes, part of the time, but frequently those eyes wander, going down the rows of singers behind her, just looking at the faces, and watching the singing. When all sat down she sat, too, a little later than the others, wanting to stand as long as she could to see what was going on. She watched it all intently, like a little religious sponge wanting to draw in every sip.

Then at sermon time she watched seriously, quietly, and without expression, just absorbing pastor Bill's introduction and the children's home presentation. I don't think she heard a word, but she must have heard the Word.

After church she basked in the greetings from Christian siblings whose names she'll never know, but was simply delighted when one of them looked familiar, "Why, I know you!" We worked our way through the clusters waiting for the dinner to begin, greeted our way out, and went to the car.

So far as I know, that was it: the greetings that made her feel like a real person again—a welcomed and valued and independent woman. It was the being there and watching it all take place around her—an hour of watching church happen—and a single sentence from the bulletin: "This church is a community of persons who believe in Jesus Christ as our Savior and Lord."

That's all it took.

December 26, 1996: *Christmas Eve and Noticing*

I'm learning a lot about memory and perception from watching my mom's journey. I know little about how these gifts work, but I sure have more appreciation of them.

When we went to church Christmas Eve, where she's been many, many times, Betty said, "I've never been here before! How pretty!" As I drove her back to her home afterward, she said, "I've never been on this street before, have I?" I said, "Yes, mom, but only about a hundred times." As we ate Christmas dinner in our dining room yesterday she looked with interest at a lovely pottery chalice made by the Makovkins, a treasure of our California days, which has been at that spot on the shelf for four years. "Is that new?" she asked.

Then she looked at me musingly, shifted her glance when she saw me notice, looked some more, and then said between hesitations, "Is it possible . . . do I see . . . is it happening that you are more bald?"

I sighed. "Yes, Mom, I've noticed that myself."

I guess you look more carefully at what's most meaningful to you. You remember that thing about the hairs of your head being numbered? By God or your mother.

MARCH 9, 1997: *At Home in Church*

Back to Trinity Church today with Betty. Along toward benediction time she said, "I feel at home here." I nodded, since Pastor McWeeny was still speaking, though quietly. There was a reflective pause, then she mused, "But I feel at home in most churches."

Blessed are the pure in heart.

Out for lunch afterward. She asked, "Where are we?" and I said, "KFC." She asked, "What does that stand for, McDonalds?" Wow, the power of advertising.

April 1, 1997: *Exciting Outing! Doctor's Office*

What does today bring? The excitement of taking my mom for a checkup with her doctor. The last time a prescription was refilled for my mom the doctor's office called to say he hadn't seen her since October, and I realized that this is the first time since she's been here that she hasn't seen him in six whole months! That's pretty remarkable, really. So we'll get out and down to see him this afternoon. Maybe she'll remember him. She certainly will when she sees him, and will pretend up a storm before then.

She's got quite an act put together, and it works great. We were at Wendy's Sunday afternoon, where we go just about every week, and she asked, "Have I been here before?" I replied, with what must have been a touch of impatience in my voice, "Yes, we come here just about every week." She responded instantly, "Yes, it's my favorite place!" From "been here before?" to "favorite place" in ten seconds flat.

April 2, 1997: *The Doctor Gets Examined*

Betty and I passed yesterday at the doctor's. We were waiting for him to come in and she asked how we picked him. I started a response: "Someone recommended him right after we moved to town eight years ago . . . ." Just then the doctor came in, heard enough of my response to know its context, and waited for me to go on, so I did: "I heard that he is young, bright, and probably wouldn't be intimidated by me."

He grinned and nodded.

Betty picked up on my language immediately and greeted the doctor with the fiercest of fake scowls: "I'm not intimidated by you!" she said.

He smiled again and said, "That's evident, Mrs. Hodges." Then he went to work. Blood pressure 122 over 72, heart and lungs fine, able to read three out of four letters of his first name, able to hear a stampeding elephant or a rampaging locomotive, able to squeeze his hands hard. All is well. When he got to filling out the annual physical exam form required by her assisted living facility, he wrote in the summary slot, "No changes."

I said to him, "At nearly ninety-one, a year with no changes is pretty close to success." He said, approvingly, "She's a wonder."

Then it was her turn to grin. I think I overestimated her doctor's ability to not be intimidated. I think she's got him.

I forgot to add that when he was poking and prodding at her she said, "I have a great body!" What self-esteem. How many others of us, one in a hundred, would make that remark? That number would not include many ballerinas, baseball players, or sky divers. Maybe Dennis Rodman.

June 11, 1997: *The New Year*

Betty continues on course. On June 1 she turned the corner into her ninety-second year. We stopped by a lovely bakery for a gigantic maple-nut cupcake before our ritual stop at Wendy's. Inside I got our coffee, stuck the candle down in the cupcake, lit it, and sang. When she recognized the song she joined in with gusto and sang with me on the last line.

She got nice cards from some of her friends and grandkids. They don't make them with 91 on them, so you have to write that in. Limited market.

When Pat and I were in Arkansas last weekend the folks that care for her reported some increased difficulty with her walking. The left leg is more wobbly, harder to work. So when we went out yesterday I watched carefully. It was not hard to see, when she had to lift her left knee with both hands to get her foot into the car and under the table at Wendy's. There's also some continued decline in speech. Sometimes she tries and tries to say it, but it's just not there. So she smiles this big broad, ingenuous grin as she gives up, as if to say, "I tried, and you'll just have to take it from there." So I do, pretty well. I've had a good deal of experience and can tell from where she's looking what she wants to talk about.

Then it will come, out of the blue, a clear question or statement carefully thought out syllable by syllable. This time, "Did I raise you right?" So I grinned and responded, "You sure tried hard enough!" She smiled and said, "I think you're all right." I replied in the same wise: "I sure try hard enough."

A pause, a sip, then, "I'm crazy about this coffee."

On the way to the car, "Can you tell I'm wobbly?" I confessed that I could. After all, it had taken us two or three minutes to exit the place, crabwise our way through the double set of heavy swinging doors, and get outside. She said, "I'm going to get rid of it."

And she'll work on it, no doubt. When that happens to me, the weakness in the left leg, the trembling when it tries to move forward, I'll be stark terrified. But she absorbs it as part of the hand life deals her and goes on coping—no big deal.

We're seeing Dr. Holdsambeck this afternoon.

• • •

I'm supposed to leave Friday for Syracuse and another General Assembly of the Presbyterian Church: "The Assembly in Search of an Issue." One will appear, or several. After all, Calvinists are not very good about drawing the line between what God is not concerned with and what he is, and we have approximately 7,684 subjects to consider, each well documented. Any of them could explode or expand or inflate to galactic significance. I'll be providing color commentary this year on the Voiceline 800 number to supplement the news reports. So I'll get to poke around, listen, ask, and muse. I was raised to muse. And then to blab.

June 12, 1997: *Bits and Pieces*

Betty was a little better yesterday when we went to see her doctor. He was very thorough and gentle, testing each side of her body with push and pull exercises, watching her walk, and asking her questions.

"What's today?"

"Tuesday."

"That's close, just one off. Can you say, 'Too hot to taste?'"

"Hot to taste."

"Can you say 'Mary had a little lamb?'"

"That's silly."

"Say it anyway."

"Muhry hadda lamb . . ."

"Is it summer, winter, spring, or fall?"

"Summer." She fooled him, but I think it was a guess.

"And how has the weather been? Hot? Warm? Or rainy?" (It has been unseasonably, unusually cold and rainy, with the farmers really concerned about puddles in their cotton fields.)

"The weather is just beautiful!" He grinned; there's that optimism again. Reach for the positive when in doubt.

We talked some more, and he told us the evidence was consistent with her having had a little stroke. Since it's recent, there may continue to be some improvement, so he didn't schedule tests or additional treatment. He told both of us that his major worry is that she might fall because of her new wobbliness. We had the danger confirmed on our way back to the car, when her left foot wouldn't step up to match the right one, so she gracefully and gently sat down on the sidewalk. Each part of her slid downward as I tried to grab it. A nice woman driving by in her van screeched to a halt, got out, and came over to help me help her up; then the two of us helped her back to the car. It could have been much worse. So narrow a line, such a razor's edge, when walking out to the car from the doctor's office can be a matter, literally, of life or death. A broken hip, at ninety-one years old, is very serious business.

On the drive back she asked, "Are you having as good a time as I am?"

I reassured her that I was. Every time is precious.

Chapter 5

Approach to
the Summit

Prelude

As this is written it does not give the end of Betty's story on this side of the River of Life. Perhaps that is at it should be, leaving the reader in that indeterminate state most of us go through when we have an aging and fragile loved one in our life whose resources are flimsy and whose reserves are almost exhausted. There is a day-to-dayness of our relationship, an eternal and acute temporariness. We never know that if we leave for the night a call will not come from the nursing station. We never know when a TV program, a meal, or a book will be interrupted by the final call. And that means more appreciation, more savoring of each moment of the precious present. That appreciation, if it can be nurtured, may serve to hold at bay the guilt of that other feeling, that other feeling of wondering how long the task must continue until the finish line appears.

We argue, since it does no good, about how we'd like to die: fast or slow, a gradual process of relinquishment or a sudden step into the street or a sudden gasp in the tennis game. A lovers' game is agonizing about who should go first. Do I want to leave my beloved with the pain of processing my departure and living through the endless consequences, while I take the purportedly "quick and easy" ticket of dying as my part of the transaction? Or is it better and more heroic to stay around and fill out the confounded insurance papers and do the grieving? No matter that such conundrums are insoluble, they can cause a tear or two.

Part of caring for an aging parent or grandparent or other loved person is how long it takes to say good-bye. Sometimes, of course, there is a measured and gradual decline, down the slanted line toward zero, month by month and day by day. With others, an exclamation point is dropped into the middle of the sentence—willy-nilly, bang, that's that.

Sometime along the line you say good-bye. Once, a dozen times. You do it alone during the long night watch by the hospital bed, or you do it as you walk in the mall and imagine what it will be like to walk by yourself. You imagine yourself into a time when you don't have to wake up every morning, aware of your elder-care responsibility, planning what your task is for the day, your obligations for this coming week. Good-bye takes a long, long time.

What this has been is an exercise, a test, a riddle: What's the essence of this woman? The exercise has consisted of stripping away each of the layers in turn, past the pride and pretense to the essence, the core, past the underwear of the soul. All that remains is a kind and gentle spirit, a positive attitude, an indomitable will, and that smile.

As this is written, we do not know when the story will end, but we know how it will end. It will be fine.

JUNE 30, 1997: *Sudden Strike*

Betty Hodges is in the hospital, all her energy depleted like last summer's beach ball in the corner of a closet. She'd been valiantly struggling each day to recover from the little stroke of last month, and to avoid the dreaded walker. Then Sunday she went lethargic on them; she wouldn't eat and complained of a stomachache. When she didn't wake up on Monday feeling any better, I took her to her doctor, who prescribed one of the "twenty-three-hour admissions" that Medicare will accept fairly easily, for tests and assessment. They've done a lot of tests today. She's still very apathetic, able only to nod yes or no, and that only occasionally. But she smiles when I come in the door.

Took me about an hour to get a half cup of soup down her tonight, but the entirety of the little smidgen of orange sherbet. More when I know more.

JULY 1, 1997: *The Day She Nearly Died*

It is pneumonia, "The Friend of the Elderly." Betty's doctor said, "If I were a prophet, I'd predict she will not survive this." But he is no prophet, only a very good doctor, so he is treating her conservatively and gently. Oxygen at six liters per minute, an IV for fluids. If she were coughing, the doctor said the prospects would be better, but she is lying very quietly, with no evident discomfort, and sleeps most of the time. Blood pressure is low, pulse is rapid. She had a high temperature this morning and was red in the face when I first saw her, but they got the fever down, so she seems quite comfortable. The nurses left us alone this afternoon, so I wept and held her hand and talked and talked. I will not abridge her privacy by telling what I said, but it was vacuous, banal, and had no style whatsoever, not the way she raised me.

I took her rings off in case there is a journey. I didn't even know there was anything left of the wedding ring, but there it was, a little wisp of white gold, almost worn away with sixty-nine years of love—love that missed not a beat when the one who gave it to her died thirty years ago.

Once she roused, opened her eyes, and looked at me fair and full, without a word: I wondered if I would decide she was looking through me, seeing all my flaws and faults and assessing me as damaged goods. I decided her look meant she was fairly content with her sixty-seven years of push and polish and prayer, and that there was little more she needed to do with me.

The nurse came in at 4:30 to check her, leaned close and spoke very loudly: "How are you, Mrs. Hodges?" Betty slowly turned and replied just as loudly and very clearly: "Very well!" No uncertainty there.

July 2, 1997: *Not So Yet*

When I went into Betty's room at 10:00 this morning, she was sitting up in the bed talking to the nurse. Actually, she was arguing, telling the young woman named Twi that there was no reason for that machine to beep at her just because she bent her elbow. Twi, who must have had about six or seven years of English, was undergunned against Betty's nine decades of using the stuff. She tried to explain that the machine was putting fluid into her arm and that when she bent it, it prevented that from happening. Not convinced.

Betty was alert, blood pressure up to 118 over 78, oxygen level at 96 percent, no fever. I fed her a good lunch. We great chefs do our best work improvising, so I improvised a low-calorie, salt-free, bland, no-taste pizza. You do that by dipping the cold white toast into the flavorless salt-free tomato soup and feeding it to her. "Just like pizza!" I bragged. She shook her head violently and rolled her eyes. That woman is sick, not crazy. Ate all the toast, and half the soup, drank the cranberry cocktail and half the milk, and ate all of the ice cream.

I'm talking to the doctor after a while and will report his no doubt lame explanation for the turnaround. But I know we heard the angel wings yesterday, on their way to someone else.

She said to me, "I was waiting for you all day yesterday. I wanted to go to church." I said, "You nearly went to heaven." She widened her eyes: "Really?" I said, "Really." She thought about that a bit, then "It would have been all right if I'd gone to heaven." I agreed. Then I said, "But you got a lot better!" She nodded, "I worked at it!"

Right. Miles to go, and all that.

July 2, 1997: *Starting Over Over*

She's out of serious danger, for now. The doctor wants her to go into a rehab place for breathing treatments and continuing oxygen therapy, and to try to get her mobile. The attempt will be to get her back into her assisted living place, rather than a nursing home. So he'll find a Medicare bed as soon as he can.

Meantime, I saw her looking appraisingly at me today, and she said, "You need a haircut." I was tempted to say, "Look, woman, we've been saving your life for the last couple of days, and that takes quite a bit of time. Yesterday it was 'Going to heaven' and today it's 'Get a haircut.' Doesn't take long to change your tune!" So I said, "I'll try to get one tomorrow."

July 9, 1997

Betty is back in the same penal colony where she served before. They'll work hard on reforming her, poor dear. A Medicare bed opened up at one of our good rehab hospitals, so Tuesday we took her over there, got her checked in, and started her on a regimen of practice in breathing, standing, eating, talking, and telling what day it is and who is the president. It is strong medicine and they're very good at it, but it's not much fun. She was at the same place a year and a half ago after a light stroke, and they got her ready for the very comfortable assisted living place she's been since then. But she sure didn't like it very much.

The cavalry has arrived, however, in the person of her stalwart eldest grandson, my son, Bruce, from New York City, and he is so good with her and with me. He managed one side of Betty, getting her into and out of wheelchair, car, wheelchair, and bed en route to rehab, and has managed nearly all sides of his father, including hosting me in his bedroom last night for drinks, snacks, and the All-Star game. Lord, it's good to be off duty for a while, just a little while.

So we're okay, for now. Again.

July 10, 1997

Bruce left today for Atlanta and then his home in New York. So I experience the parent-child business from the other end of the telescope at the same time, first this way, then the other. I remember this so well, so well, from times when I was thirty or forty and went home to visit the folks. It was a lark, a sport, a trifle, a bagatelle, a pleasant diversion in midsummer, a nice trip for the kids to see their grandparents and to show off. When we left it was forgotten at the city limits, back to the real world, start the clock again.

But for them, I now understand, it was like tearing out a bit of flesh right around the heart, when we left.

July 14, 1997: *The New Baseline*

Betty's situation remains virtually unchanged. She sits quietly most of the time, sleeps a lot, and is very apathetic. She responds only rarely, and then in monosyllables. It takes two attendants to get her up to practice walking, and her appetite is still poor. However, I took her a *USA Today* and read half a dozen stories to her since she's been a voracious newspaper reader since birth. After each article I asked, "Do you like that?" and "Want another?" She nodded insistently each time.

Then I put the little potted daisy Bruce brought her in her lap. She reached for a stalk to check it out, since she's always detested plastic flowers, and that warm and loving smile crossed her face. That $2.49 gift continues to give.

JULY 26, 1997

I showed her new pictures of her great-grandchildren, including Jarred's first baseball card, looking just like one for the big guys. He is holding a bat that's bigger than he is, with his statistics on the back: Jarred Hodges, age 4, weight 48, Bay City Little League, Coach Shroeder. It doesn't give his batting average, alas. I'm gonna turn down a stone million dollars for that card twenty years from now. Or then again, maybe I'll sell. What a great idea some enterprising photographer had: baseball cards for little leaguers.

I am still angry at this stuff that is taking Betty piece by piece. There's still some good stuff there, like that smile I got when I came in yesterday after my three days away. But we're getting close to the core.

AUGUST 4, 1997: *Routine Survival*

We're settling into a routine. I think they did that at Auschwitz, too, to make survival possible. Betty sits in her chair, looking pleasantly out the door and down the hall, or sleeps with her eyes half open, or looks up at the TV, without change of expression. I don't think she can hear the sound, and her roommate is adept at the remote control, providing a good deal of variety, none of interest to anyone over eight. When I come in to see her her expression brightens, and she speaks a phrase. Then I get another sentence or two with my initial questions, "How are you?" "I'm fine today!" "Are you all right?" "Yes, I'm all right." But when I get more complicated than that, "What did you do today? What did you have for lunch? Do we need to talk about anything?" she lapses into the pleasant expression, perhaps nodding, but without words. Her eyes keep stealing upward to the TV. When I leave I get "I love you, too" in answer to mine and a nod at, "See you tomorrow."

She's traveling fast and light, interested in very little in this world, but she's content and serene. Oh, thank God for that. I went by her former residence, the very comfortable room in the assisted living home, where she was until July 1, and got her clothes, pictures, jewelry, and all the Christmas presents she's gotten in the past two years—the powder, lotion, Crayolas, and stuff, all unused. There was a whole drawer full of every Christmas card and birthday card she could squirrel away and of all the church bulletins and church newsletters people have been sending her. In total, it didn't fill the trunk and backseat of the Oldsmobile. "Free from all worldly cares and possessions," just free. It doesn't matter, any of it.

I marked with her initials the things she can use in the new setting, sweats and slacks and tops. I have carefully put away those magnificent handmade sweaters with the "From the Needles of Betty Hodges" labels in them (they never wear out) and have boxed the opera dress; the dress from Susan's wedding; the stylish three-piece summer dress, fit for the Queen's garden party; all the lovely lingerie, nothing there for old ladies, beautiful frilly lacy slips and petticoats. All are put away safe and sound.

They dress her carefully and creatively in the rehab place, sometimes a top in garish color warfare with the bottom, and sometimes a summer top with winter pants. She never remarks, complains, or seems to notice, however, that stylish fashion plate with her immaculate taste.

There is a lovely Rossetti poem I hear in a new way:

But dreaming through the twilight
That doth not rise nor set
Haply I may remember
And haply may forget.

August 13, 1997: *Special Treatment*

Betty is in a state-of-the-heart treatment center, with most of the lifesaving machinery currently available, and all kinds of devices to refurbish banged-up and worn-out people. Yesterday she underwent a sophisticated and delicate advanced procedure aimed at restoring functioning and self-image. She had her hair done.

I was permitted to watch this arcane procedure, called shampoo and set, for the very first time in my life. It was quite an experience to be allowed into a specially equipped chamber with all kinds of mysterious machines and devices. It is evidently quite unusual for persons of my sort to be allowed inside, though everyone was extremely polite.

The person in charge, called the Operator, was adept, facile, and extremely capable. She showed her advanced level of competence by speaking constantly as she worked on subjects totally without reference to what her fingers were doing. She seemed to shift her hands into automatic.

A number of others undergoing different procedures were seated around the chamber in various stages of completion. They seemed to be generally content, regardless of the quite extreme measures that had been applied to their heads, and they appeared to be immobilized and perhaps tranquilized by large plastic globe-like helmets that came down over their heads and hummed to keep them quiet.

After the hair was sensuously laved, lathered, and rinsed, Berta, the Operator, combed it smooth as spun silver, placid in her fingers. Then she skillfully chose a requisite amount of hair, judged flawlessly to be enough, and spun that swath around a hollow plastic tube, fixing it with a cunningly designed aluminum clip. She continued the process over the whole head, front to back, crown to neck. There seemed to be a platonic order to the process, as her fingers knew exactly the number of rolls required.

Once done, the roll-bedecked head was placed beneath a dome to keep it quiet, while the Operator turned her attention to another supplicant.

My mother sat content and still, smiling quietly, as if aware she was part of a ritual of eternal meaning that has been done since shortly after the dawn of time.

Later, when the dome stopped humming, the Operator turned to Betty again. Like lightning, her fingers retraced the rolls, removing each pin, releasing the blue cylinders. A head covered with rolls of silver remained. Then, with facile ease, a comb, a brush, and a number of specialized instruments, the tight rolls were loosened, the hair smooth-brushed to a silver mane, which was then sculpted in tiny touches to a crown of beauty. Touched, combed, lifted, patted, smoothed.

Berta had asked me earlier if my mother wore it teased, and I had no idea what that meant. I'd gone to the phone to ask Pat, who said with exasperation, "She has to tease it some because it's so long." I repeated that and Berta nodded in acknowledgment of that arcane woman code. She then reached into the mass of hair with a clever plastic forklike probe and fluffed up hair to little puffs, which were then smoothed over with the brush.

Toward the end there was obvious effort at uniqueness and creativity. The Operator would assess, step back, and muse, then touch with a comb, and a whorl appeared. She'd spray, then comb, then spray again. An upsweep there, downsweep here, and the ritual was completed. She moved my mother's wheelchair to the mirror and stepped back. Betty responded with the appropriate ritualistic antiphon: "It looks good!" with a broad, broad smile. The Operator nodded in satisfaction.

You should have seen her smile as I wheeled her back to her room, through the day room, by the knot of women around the nursing station, and by the dining room with those awaiting supper. I could see the eyes of all we passed looking on with envy and admiration.

We have a permanent ordered in two weeks. It's something like an advanced degree.

SEPTEMBER 6, 1997: *Next Stop?*

Betty is the same—pleasant, dopey, smiling, fragile, and so very thin. I told her that Pat and I would probably skip church, sleep in, and loaf tomorrow. She shook her head sternly, then said, "I'll have to get after you!" First unsolicited comment in days. The Sabbath gorgon, on duty. Then later, "I want to know . . ." I tried to finish it for her, but without success. "How long you'll be here?" Head shake. "How much it costs?" Head shake, then laughter. "Why you're here?" Head shake. "Where you're going next?" She threw back her head and laughed.

I read her the front page news about Diana, and told her Teresa's funeral would be Saturday. "How old was she?" she asked. "Eighty-seven," I said. The headshake again, and I swear it meant regret that Teresa wasn't able to live out her full span. "Two funerals," she said, with the rueful headshake. Great tragedies get through, even through that nearly impenetrable fog.

She had a coughing spell Thursday morning, quite severe. Afterwards, the respiratory therapy people had to come suction out her breathing passages to head off aspiration pneumonia. By the time I came Thursday afternoon she was fine. She had vehemently and convincingly shaken her head when they asked her if she wanted to let me know about the coughing spell. She was afraid I'd put her in the hospital; that's why, I know. She's been down that path before and knows where it leads.

But she was fine today, able to mourn the two younger women who died this week.

SEPTEMBER 12, 1997

Where would you be if you had no way to finish the sentence, "I want to say I'm ...."? That's where Betty is. She has worked *very* hard at her speech therapy, and Ina is pleased that they've come so far from the mostly nods, and head-shakes, smiles, and frowns. But there is still so much erosion from where she was prior to July 1. There are some standard phrases that come pretty easily: "Isn't that pretty?" and "I'm wonderful!" But phrases with options or modifiers are hard.

So she tried four or five times today to finish it, "I want to say I'm ... brbbr." "I'm ... brrbb." "I'm bBBrb!" The she gave up helplessly, looked at me with that smile, and shook her head in frustration.

I tried to help, "Do you want to tell me how you are?" Head nodding affirmatively. "Are you ... worried, troubled, afraid, bothered, fine ..." All I had to do was get that far, and she picked up on it: "I'm fine!"

"Good." I said, "I hope so."

There was another subject very much on her mind. I could see her thinking to find the words very, very intentionally, and then it came: "When will we have ... the book?"

Ah yes, the book, this book. Of course. "In June," I told her. I nearly went on to finish it with that marketing-oriented completer, "In time for General Assembly."

Then it came to me, the real answer, so I saved myself quite narrowly from error: "In June," I said, "For your birthday."

She nodded with satisfaction. "That will be fine."